Welcome to Issue Twelve

End to End

XTB stands for **eXplore The Bible**.

Read a bit of the Bible each day and...
- Check out the very first Easter in **John's Gospel**.
- Meet **Daniel** and **Nehemiah** as we finish the story of the Old Testament.
- Then read about heaven in the last book in the Bible—**Revelation**.

Are you ready to explore the Bible? Fill in the bookmark...
...then turn over the page to start exploring with XTB!

Sometimes I'm called

.... (nickname)

My birthday is

....

My age is

....

One thing I'm looking forward
to in heaven is

....

....

Table Talk FOR FAMILIES

Look out for **Table Talk** — a book to help children and
adults explore the Bible together. It can be used by:
- Families
- One adult with one child
- Children's leaders with their groups
- Any other way you want to try

Table Talk uses the same Bible passages as XTB so that they can be used together if wanted.
You can buy Table Talk from your local Good Book Company website:

UK: www.thegoodbook.co.uk • North America: www.thegoodbook.com
Australia: www.thegoodbook.com.au • New Zealand: www.thegoodbook.co.nz

How to find your way around the Bible.

Look out for the **READ** sign.
It tells you what Bible bit to read.

So, if the notes say... READ Daniel 1v1-9
...this means chapter 1 and verses 1 to 9
...and this is how you find it.

Use the **Contents** page in your Bible to
find where Daniel begins.

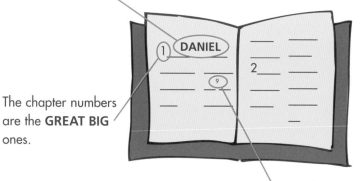

The chapter numbers
are the **GREAT BIG**
ones.

The verse numbers are the
tiny ones!

Oops! Keep getting lost?
Cut out this bookmark and use it to keep your place.

How to use xtb

1  Find a time and place when you can read the Bible each day.

2  Get your Bible, a pencil and your XTB notes.

3  Ask God to help you to understand what you read.

4  Read today's XTB page and Bible bit.

5 Pray about what you have read and learnt.

6  If you can, talk to an adult or a friend about what you've learnt.

Your Free XTB Bible Timeline

This copy of XTB comes with a free **XTB Bible Timeline**.

HISTORY = HIS STORY
Bible history is **His** story—**God's** story. Your Bible Timeline shows God's amazing plan for His people, from the very beginning of time to the very end. It shows how God has made and kept amazing promises to His people—and the fantastic future we have to look forward to with Jesus in heaven!

Are you ready to dip into your Bible Timeline?
Then hurry on to Day 1.

DAY 1 HANDY HISTORY

Grab your **XTB Bible Timeline** and use it to fill in the gaps.

> Kingdom of Israel **d**_____
> then sent into **e**_____

D_____

HISTORY = H_____ **S**_____

Ahem! Attention please!
It's time for a handy
history lesson...

- The Israelites used to live in <u>one</u> kingdom, called Israel. Their kings were Saul, David and Solomon.
- But then the kingdom was divided into <u>two</u>:
  —the biggest chunk was still called **Israel**.
  —the smaller bit was called **Judah**.
- God warned the people in **Israel** that if they <u>turned away</u> from Him, they would be <u>turned out</u> of their country.
  —but they didn't listen!

- So God allowed the **Assyrians** to capture Israel, and take the people away into exile (which means being sent away from your home and country).
- God also warned the people of **Judah** that the same thing would happen to <u>them</u> if they zigzagged away from God —but they didn't listen either!
- So God allowed the **Babylonians** to zoom in and capture Judah, and take the people far away to Babylon.

*Copy all the **red letters** (in order) to discover the name of the Babylonian king.*

King _ _ _ _ _ _ _ _ _ _ _ _ _ _

Turn to the next page to find out more.

WHO'S THE KING?

READ
Daniel 1v1-9

King Nebuchadnezzar wanted some of the young men from Judah to be trained to serve him. But King Neb was very fussy! What were they to be like? (v3-4)

old

ugly

healthy

good looking   lazy

young

sick   from royal or noble families

quick at learning

How long were they to be trained for? (v5)

_____ **years**

King Nebuchadnezzar was rich and powerful, and ruled over the huge Babylonian empire. He <u>seemed</u> to be the most powerful king around...

BUT check out v2 again.
Who gave Judah and its king into Nebuchadnezzar's hands???

The _____

Who made the Babylonian official sympathetic (kind) to Daniel? (v9)

_____

HISTORY = HIS STORY

As we read the book of Daniel we will meet three very powerful kings. But they all had to learn that **God** is the **Real King** of everyone and everything. <u>He</u> is in charge!

God is the Real King!

PRAY

Dear God, thank You that You are the Real King of everyone and everything. Please help me to learn more about You as I read the book of Daniel. Amen

DAY 2 THE BEST OF THE BUNCH

 Daniel 1v8-21

Daniel and his three friends have been captured by the Babylonians. They're being trained to serve King Nebuchadnezzar. But there's a problem! *Use the **Veggie Code** to see what it is.*

Daniel won't __ __ __ the king's __ __ __ __

We don't know exactly what was wrong with the royal food and wine. But Daniel thought he'd be offending God if he ate it. So he refused to eat it!

The Babylonians could have been very angry. But check yesterday's XTB page to see **who** made the Babylonian official kind to Daniel.

Daniel suggested a kind of test. For ten days, he and his friends would only eat...

__ __ __ __ __ __ __ __ __

At the end of the ten days, the Babylonian official would check to see if they looked healthy or not.

Veggie Code

 = A
 = B
 = D
 = E
 = F
 = G
 = I
 = K
 = L
 = O
 = S
 = T
 = V

READ
Daniel 1v15-21

Were Daniel and co. healthy? (v15)

Yes / No

What did God give Daniel? (v17)
a) Knowledge and the ability to have dreams.
b) Knowledge and the ability to understand dreams.
c) Knowledge and the ability to understand French.

At the end of three years, King Neb tested everyone who had been trained, and chose the best of the bunch to serve him. Who did he choose? (v19)

a) Daniel
b) Daniel, Hananiah, Mishael and Azariah
c) Daniel, Harry, Michael and Alexander

THINK+PRAY

King Neb chose the best of the bunch—but it was **God** who gave them their abilities! (v17) What are you good at? (*Maths, sport, cheering people up...*) It's God who gives us all our abilities. Thank Him, and ask Him to help you use your abilities to serve Him.

DAY 3 BAD DREAMS

 Daniel 2v1-18

King Neb had a bad dream. He had no idea what it meant. But he had lots of advisers, whose job was to answer difficult questions—so he called them in to explain the dream...

READ
Daniel 2v1-4

Fill in the gaps from v3-4

I've had a **d**_____ that troubles me. I want to know what it **m**_____.

T_____ us your dream and we will interpret (explain) it.

But it wasn't going to be that easy! King Neb <u>refused</u> to tell them his dream.

Tell me the dream. Then I will know that you can also tell me what it means.

But they couldn't do it! Nobody knew what the king had dreamt.

King Neb was furious! He ordered that all of his advisers must be...

— — — — — —

Use yesterday's code.

<u>All</u> of the king's advisers were to be killed—including Daniel and his friends!

READ
Daniel 2v14-18

What did Daniel tell his friends to do? (v18)
a) Run away
b) Get ready to fight
c) Pray to God for help

How do you think God answered their prayers? *We'll find out tomorrow...*

THINK + PRAY

If you find yourself in a tricky situation... PRAY! Take your troubles to God and ask Him to help you. Get your friends to pray for you too. God longs to hear us talk to Him and He loves to answer our prayers. Are you worried about anything at the moment? Tell God about it now, and ask Him to help you.

VISIONS AND DREAMS

King Nebuchadnezzar was angry! Nobody could tell him his dream. So he ordered that all of his advisers must be killed!

But Daniel and his friends knew that **God** is the **Real King** of everyone and everything. So they prayed to God for help...

READ
Daniel 2v19

Wow! Daniel had a dream too—in which God showed him everything he needed to know to help King Neb.

How do you think Daniel felt?

Daniel thanked and praised God...

READ
Daniel 2v20-23

Praise God for **ever** and ever.
He is **wise** and powerful.
He changes the **times** and seasons.
He makes and unmakes **kings**.
He gives **wisdom** and knowledge.
He reveals **secrets** that are deep and hidden.
I **thank** and **praise** You, God of my ancestors.
You have made known to me the **dream** of the king.

Fit all of the <u>blue words</u> into the puzzle. The yellow boxes will show two new words.

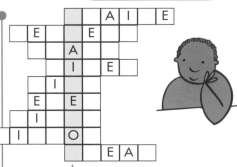

P_____ G_____

THINK + PRAY

What can <u>you</u> praise and thank God for?

1_____

2_____

3_____

Thank and praise God for these things now.

DAY 5 SMASHING STATUE

Daniel went to see King Nebuchadnezzar.

No man can tell you what you dreamt.

But there is a God in heaven who reveals mysteries.

You saw an enormous dazzling statue.

The head of the statue was made of pure gold.

Its chest and arms were of silver.

Its legs were of iron.

Then you saw a rock, which hit the statue.

Its middle and thighs were of bronze.

And its feet partly of iron and partly of clay.

The statue was broken into pieces and blew away

But the rock became a huge mountain and filled the whole earth.

READ Daniel 2v36-45

King Neb's dream was about the **future**.

• King Neb was the head of gold. He and his kingdom were strong and powerful—but only because **God** gave them that power! (v37)
• After them would come several more kingdoms.
• Each would be less powerful than the one before.
• The last kingdom would be divided.

The rock in the dream stands for a kingdom that will last for <u>ever</u>. It was set up by the **G_____ of h_____** (v44)

The rock was the start of this great kingdom. The rock was actually a <u>person</u> who God sent to be King. Check out the **big red block** on your **Bible Timeline** to see who it was.

PRAY Jesus is the King of the universe. His kingdom will rule for ever! If you're a Christian (a follower of Jesus) then you're a part of that amazing kingdom! How does that make you feel? Talk to God about it now.

DAY 6 — HOW HIGH???

God had helped Daniel to explain the king's dream to him. As a result, King Neb learnt something very important about God. *Cross out the **X**s to see what it was.*

Your God is the **XGRXEAXTEXSTX** of gods and the **XLXORXDX** of **XKXINXGSX**. (Daniel 2v47)

Yippee! It looks like King Neb had got his thinking right at last. He knew that **God** is the <u>Real King</u>.

But then he did something very wrong...

READ
Daniel 3v1

King Neb built a HUGE gold statue.

• How **high** was it? (v1) _____

• How **wide** was it? (v1) _____

King Neb gathered all the most important people in the country and forced them to bow down and worship the statue. Anyone who refused would be thrown into a blazing furnace!

Daniel and his friends knew that **God** is the Real King. It would be very wrong to worship anyone or anything else. Daniel's friends—Shadrach, Meshach and Abdenego (we'll call them S,M&A!)—were in the crowd in front of the statue. But they <u>refused</u> to bow down to it!

READ
Daniel 3v13-18

The God we serve is **XAXBLXEX** to **XSAXVEX** us.

But even if He does not, we will **XNOXTX** serve your gods or worship the gold statue **XYOXUX** have set up.

PRAY

S,M&A knew that God could save them from the flames. But even if He didn't, they were determined to put God first, and not bow down to a statue! Do <u>you</u> want to put God first in your life? Then ask Him to help you, even when it's very hard.

DAY 7 FACING THE FIRE

Quick Quiz

(Draw lines to match each question and answer.)

1 What did King Neb build?

2 What did he order the people to do?

3 What would happen if anyone disobeyed?

4 Who refused to worship the statue?

5 Why wouldn't S,M&A bow to a statue?

A S,M&A (Shadrach, Meshach and Abednego).

B A huge gold statue.

C Because God is the Real King.

D Worship the gold statue.

E They'd be thrown into a blazing furnace!

King Neb was furious with S,M&A. He ordered the furnace to be made seven times hotter than usual. Then S,M&A were tied up and thrown in!!!

READ
Daniel 3v19-27

Answers: 1B, 2D, 3E, 4A, 5C

Fill in the chart by using verses 24-25.

What King Neb expected	What actually happened
Three men in the furnace	_____ men
Firmly tied up	
All three to be dead	

Wow! A man appeared in the furnace with S,M&A. All four were walking around in the fire—untied and unharmed!

God doesn't always save Christians like this. BUT He sent Jesus to rescue <u>all</u> Christians from <u>the worst</u> danger ever. *(More about this on Day 30.)*

THINK + PRAY

God <u>does</u> allow hard things to happen (often to teach us something) but He is always **with us**, and will **help us** when we ask. Is anything bad or sad worrying you? Talk to God about it, and ask Him to help you. He will!

THE GOD WHO RESCUES

Shadrach, Meshach and Abednego had been thrown into the blazing furnace. But they weren't hurt. They didn't even smell of smoke!

King Nebuchadnezzar was amazed! *Take the first letter of each pic to see what he said about God.*

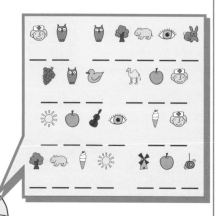

*Grab your **Bible Timeline** to check out three things about the God who rescues.*

1 About 600BC (Daniel on Timeline)

King Neb had been <u>sure</u> that his furnace would kill S,M&A...

What _ _ _ will be able

to _ _ _ _ _ _ _ you

from my hand? (v15)

But now he knew that everything S,M&A had told him about God was true.

READ
Daniel 3v28-30

King Neb was right that only **God** could rescue His people like this. But God was going to do an even more amazing rescue...

2 About 30AD (Red block on Timeline)

Who lived, died and came back to life again as our Rescuer?

We'll find out more about how Jesus rescues us when we start reading John's Gospel on Day 21.

3 Today (After 2000AD on Timeline)

Christians are people who have been rescued by Jesus and follow Him as their King. They look forward to living with Jesus in heaven.

PRAY

If you're a Christian, thank God for sending Jesus as your Rescuer. If you're not sure, ask God to help you to find out more as you read His Word, the Bible.

DAY 9 — STUMPED BY A DREAM

The next chapter of Daniel was written by King Neb himself! He tells us about a frightening dream he had. No one could explain it, so he turned to Daniel (who he called Belteshazzar).

READ
Daniel 4v9-18

Circle the correct answers

The tree was
tiny/huge/ugly
(v10)

The tree
grew/shrunk/faded
big and strong and reached the
sky/moon/sun (v11)

Its
leaves/branches/apples were
beautiful. (v12)

Birds/Monkeys/Cats lived in its branches. (v12)

People/Fish/Animals sheltered under it. (v12)

But an
angel/pigeon/child
said the tree must be cut down. (v14)

Only the stump would be left, with a band of
gold/iron/wood
and bronze. (v15)

The tree in the dream was a picture of a <u>person</u>. He would be cut down from his powerful position and become like an animal! He would live outside among the plants until seven years had passed (v15-16).

Fit your <u>answers</u> into the puzzle.

What do the yellow boxes spell?

PRAY

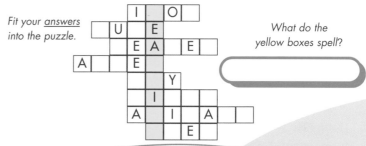

Verse 17 says that God is the
Real King (sovereign). That means God is in control of everything. He has the power to do anything at all! If you mean it, thank God that He's in charge of YOUR life too.

DAY 10 PRIDE AND PREJUDICE

Do you remember King Neb's dream of a huge tree that was cut down?
Follow the lines to see what each part meant.

A huge, strong tree

The tree was cut down

A stump was left

Neb will become king again

King Neb was hugely powerful

Neb will become a dancer

Neb would be cut down from his powerful position

Daniel warned King Neb what his dream meant. But King Neb was too <u>proud</u> to do anything about it…

Look how great Babylon is! **I** built it to display **my** power and might, **my** glory and majesty.

Before he'd even finished speaking, King Neb heard a voice from heaven telling him that his dream was now going to come true!

READ
Daniel 4v28-33

It happened exactly as God had said. King Neb was kicked out of Babylon and lived like a wild animal, eating grass. He even started to look like an animal!

THINK + PRAY

King Neb was too <u>proud</u>. He knew his own power was given to him by God (Daniel 2v37), that God is the 'Lord of kings' (2v47) and God had rescued S,M&A from the blazing furnace (3v28). BUT King Neb still thought he was more important than anyone else—even God! Pride is wrong, because **God** is the greatest and **He's** the One in control of everything. Tell God about any times you've been proud. Say sorry and ask Him to help you change.

DAY 11 KING OF KINGS

King Nebuchadnezzar lived like an animal for seven years. He even ate grass! Then God gave him his mind back—and he praised God as the King of Kings...

READ
Daniel 4v34-37

*Use the **crown code** to see what King Neb had learnt about God.*

Crown Code

👑 = A
👑 = E
👑 = G
👑 = H
👑 = I
👑 = L
👑 = M
👑 = N
👑 = O
👑 = R
👑 = S
👑 = T
👑 = V
👑 = W
👑 = Y

- God's rule (dominion) is for _ _ _ _

- God's kingdom lasts for _ _ _ _   _ _ _ _ _ _ _

- God does what He wants— _ _ _ _ _ can stop Him!

- Everything God does is _ _ _ _ _

- God is _ _ _ _ _ _ _ _ just (fair)

Neb became king again—just as God said he would. In fact, he was even more powerful than he was before! But this time, King Neb used his power to tell everyone about God. *Read the beginning of chapter 4 to see what he told people.*

READ
Daniel 4v1-3

You and I aren't in charge of huge empires! So we can't write a letter to everyone and then insist that they read it—which is what King Neb could do!
BUT if we tell God that we want to tell other people about Him—even if we also tell Him that we're really scared, and will need lots of help!—then God will give us the opportunities to tell people about Him.

What happened with that hassle at school?

Well, er, I talked to God about it and an amazing thing happened...

PRAY
If you really want to tell other people about God, then tell Him so now, and ask Him to help you.

WRITE AND WRONG

xtb Daniel 5v1-9

The book of Daniel now jumps ahead a few years. King Neb is dead and King Belshazzar is in charge of Babylonia.

READ
Daniel 5v1-4

Belshazzar had a huge party. What did they drink from? (v2)

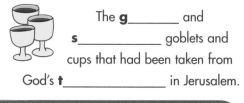

The **g_____** and **s_____** goblets and cups that had been taken from God's **t_____** in Jerusalem.

These special goblets had been made to praise the One True God.

But Belshazzar used them to praise pretend gods made of **g_____**, silver, **b_____**, iron, **w_____** and stone! (v4)

Suddenly, something frightening appeared on the wall!
Join the dots to see what it was.

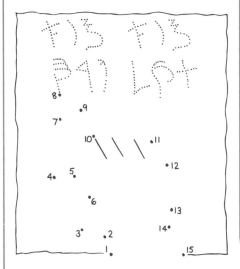

King Belshazzar was terrified!

READ
Daniel 5v5-9

How many of the king's advisers could help him? (v8) **None / A few / All**

But there was one man who <u>could</u> read the writing on the wall. *Tomorrow, **Daniel** will tell Belshazzar (and us!) what it said...*

THINK + PRAY

Belshazzar used God's special goblets to have a drunken party and worship pretend gods! I'm sure you've never done that! But have you ever disrespected God? (*Told wrong jokes? Made fun of the Bible? Messed around when someone is teaching you the Bible?*) If you have, say sorry to God. Ask Him to help you to show Him respect.

Can you read backwards???

If not, use a mirror to help you.

- King Belshazzar used the goblets from God's **temple** to drink wine and praise pretend gods.
- Suddenly a **hand** appeared and started **writing** on the wall.
- Belshazzar was **terrified**!
- None of the king's advisors could **read** the writing.
- But then **Daniel** was brought in.

Daniel reminded Belshazzar of everything that had happened to King Neb. Belshazzar <u>knew</u> these things, but he still hadn't cared about God...

READ
Daniel 5v22-28

What Belshazzar <u>did</u>:
- Praised pretend gods which cannot **see** or **hear** or **understand**

What Belshazzar <u>didn't do</u>:
- Honour the One True God who has power over his **life** and everything he **does**

The mysterious hand wrote these words:

MENE, MENE, TEKEL, PARSIN

1. Mene means **n**_____
(v26)

Belshazzar's days were <u>numbered</u>. He had sinned against God and God would punish him very soon.

2. Tekel means **w**_____
(v27)

When <u>weighed</u> and measured against God's holy and perfect standards, Belshazzar had completely failed.

---

3. Parsin means **d**_____
(v26)

Belshazzar's kingdom of Babylon was going to be <u>divided</u>. It would be taken over by the Medes and Persians.

READ
Daniel 5v29-31

God's message to Belshazzar came true that night! Belshazzar got exactly what he deserved.

Write your name backwards:

_____

PRAY The One True God has power over **your** life too! Talk to Him about how that makes you feel.

DANIEL'S HABIT

Do you have any habits?

Daniel had a habit. *Use the **pigpen code** to see what it was.*

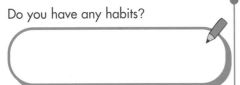

D _ _ _ _ _

_ _ _ _ _ _

pigpen code

A	D	E
I	L	N
P	R	Y

⌐ = **A**
⌐ = **D**

Sounds like a great habit. But in today's story, some wicked men use Daniel's habit to get him into trouble!

READ
Daniel 6v1-5

The new king, Darius, found that Daniel was hard-working and good at his job. So Darius wanted to put Daniel in charge of everything.

The other officials tried to get Daniel into trouble. But what was their problem? (v4)

a) Daniel had done nothing wrong
b) Daniel had done nothing right
c) Daniel had done nothing

Wow! By this time Daniel was over 80 years old. But his enemies couldn't find anything that he'd done wrong! Do you think that would be true of <u>your</u> life?

Daniel's enemies decided to set a trap for him. First, they persuaded King Darius to make a new law...

READ
Daniel 6v6-10

What a terrible law! For a whole month, no one was allowed to pray to anyone except the king. And if they did, they'd be thrown to the lions!

But what did Daniel do when he heard about the new law? (v10)

Daniel p_____

It looks like Dan's going to be in a L-O-T of trouble! *We'll find out tomorrow...*

THINK + PRAY

Daniel probably had his habit for the whole of his life. What a great habit to have! What about you? When's the best time for you to pray? If you want to have a praying habit like Daniel's, then tell God about it and ask Him to help you.

DAY 15   ROARING RESCUE

What was Daniel's habit?   **Daniel p_____**

Daniel's enemies had tricked King Darius into making a law that said no one was allowed to pray to anyone except the king. Now they were ready to trap Daniel...

READ
Daniel 6v11-16

King Darius desperately wanted to save Daniel—but even the <u>king</u> wasn't allowed to break the new law! What did he say to Daniel? (v16)

May your **G_____**, whom you serve continually, **r_____** you!

King Darius <u>couldn't</u> save Daniel—but he hoped that **God** (the Real King!) <u>could</u>.

READ
Daniel 6v17-23

Why didn't the lions eat Daniel?

a) God's angel saved Daniel — *true / false*
b) The lions weren't hungry — *true / false*
c) Daniel was innocent in God's sight — *true / false*
d) Daniel had trusted God — *true / false*
e) The lions were asleep — *true / false*

God had kept Daniel totally safe. He wasn't even scratched!

THINK SPOT

Daniel chose to keep praying to God. As a result, he got into trouble and was thrown to the lions. The same will sometimes be true for us. We will get hassle for being Christians. God won't always stop us from having trouble. But we can be sure that He will be with us and help us.

PRAY

Thank God that He's always with His people. Ask Him to help you to trust Him as Daniel did.

Answers: a—true; b—false; c—true; d—true; e—false

DAY 16 THE LIVING GOD

- Daniel's enemies set a trap to get him thrown to the lions.
- But God sent an angel to shut the lions' mouths.
- King Darius was thrilled that Daniel was safe.
- He threw Daniel's enemies to the lions instead.
- Those bad men were torn to pieces before they hit the ground! (v24)

King Darius wrote a letter to all the people in his empire. He told them all about God!

Follow the maze to see some key words from Darius' letter.

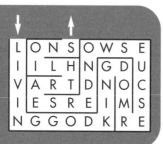

L	O	N	S	O	W	S	E
I	I	L	H	N	G	D	U
V	A	R	T	D	N	O	C
I	E	S	R	E	I	M	S
N	G	G	O	D	K	R	E

L _ _ _ _ _   G _ _

K _ _ _ _ _ _ _

R _ _ _ _ _ _ _

W _ _ _ _ _ _

L _ _ _ _ _

Look out for those words as you read the king's letter for yourself.

READ
Daniel 6v25-28

King Darius had learnt some great things about God. Now it's your turn! Write a letter **to God**, telling Him how you feel about Him and thanking Him for what He's done for you.

Dear God,

DAY 17 — DANIEL'S DREAM

Daniel 7 is a flashback, to the time when Belshazzar was king. In this chapter, Daniel tells us about a very odd dream...

READ
Daniel 7v1-8

God gave Daniel a vision (dream) of four strange beasts. *Draw a line to match each beast with its picture.*

Beast 1 (v4)

Beast 2 (v5)

Beast 3 (v6)

Beast 4 (v7)

Later on, we're told that the <u>four beasts</u> stand for <u>four different kingdoms</u> (v17).

(Like Babylonia, Persia, Greece and the Roman Empire, who were all powerful at different times.)

But these powerful kingdoms only <u>seem</u> to be in charge. In the next part of Daniel's dream, he sees the Real King...

READ
Daniel 7v9-10

Daniel saw **God** on the throne. He's the Real King. He is called the 'Ancient of Days' (your Bible may say 'One who has been living for ever'). God has <u>always</u> existed and <u>always</u> will! He rules for ever!

What did God look like? (v9)

- His clothes were **wh**_____ as **sn**_____.
- His hair was like pure, white **wo**_____.
- His throne was flaming with **fi**_____.

White is pure. God is pure and perfect. Everything He does is good and right. God is also powerful, and will punish those who go against Him. He is in total control.

PRAY

Daniel's dream is hard to understand. But one thing that's very clear is that **God** is in charge. He is the King of Kings, and will rule for ever. Thank Him for this.

DAY 18 THE SON OF MAN

Daniel is having a strange dream, with weird beasts that stand for different kingdoms, and God sitting on a throne of fire.

There's also a little horn in his dream. A horn was a picture of great power—but this horn still had far <u>less</u> power than God...

READ
Daniel 7v11-12

Take the first letter of each pic to see what this horn was a picture of.

— — — — — — — — —

This king spoke against God and made God's people suffer (v25). But **no one** is more powerful than God—so this proud king was defeated.

Then Daniel saw someone very special...

READ
Daniel 7v13-14

- One like a _ _ _ of _ _ _

'Son of Man' is the name Jesus called Himself (eg: John 9v35-37). Jesus is God's Son but He became a human being.

- He was given authority, glory and _ _ _ _ _

God made Jesus King, the ruler of everything.

- People of all _ _ _ _ _ _ _ _ _ worshipped Him.

One day, everyone will bow down to Jesus!

- His _ _ _ _ _ _ _ _ will never be destroyed.

God's fantastic kingdom will last for ever.

PRAY

Jesus wasn't just the tiny baby we remember at Christmas. He is the powerful, conquering King. He will destroy all His enemies and everyone will worship Him. Tell Jesus how great He is, and ask Him to be King of every part of your life.

DANIEL PRAYS

Use these words to fill in the gaps. →

Daniel 9v1-19

Today we get to listen in as Daniel reads the Bible and prays.

READ
Daniel 9v1-3

Daniel was reading the book of **J**_____. In it, God said Jerusalem would be in ruins for _____ years. So Daniel **p**_____ about this, while fasting (going without food) and wearing **s**_____ and ashes (to show his sadness).

Did you know?

God's people were in **exile** (sent away from Israel and Jerusalem). This was their punishment for turning away from God. But God had also promised to bring His people back home after 70 years. (This promise is in Jeremiah 29v10.)

Words box: covenant, Name, Jeremiah, prayed, 70, sackcloth, forgiving, merciful

Daniel's prayer is l-o-n-g, with some tricky words, so we're going to dip into three verses that sum it up:

READ **Daniel 9v4**

God keeps His c_____

God always keeps His promises (covenants). God promised to end the exile after 70 years—so Daniel prayed that God would keep His promise.

READ **Daniel 9v9**

God is m_____ **and**

f_____

Mercy is when God does not treat us the way we deserve. God's people had turned away from Him—but Daniel prayed that God would forgive them.

READ **Daniel 9v19**

God's N_____ **matters**

Daniel wasn't just praying for himself and his people. It mattered to him that **God** got the respect and glory He deserved.

Tomorrow we'll see how Daniel's prayer was answered...

THINK + PRAY

When Daniel read God's promise, he started praying straight away. Do the things you read in the Bible make you pray straight away? To say sorry to God or to thank Him for what you've learnt? Why not try it, starting RIGHT NOW!

Daniel has been asking God to keep His promise to bring His people back home to Jerusalem. Straight away God sent an angel to give Daniel His answer...

READ
Daniel 9v20-23

What was the angel called? (v21) **G**_____

How quickly did God answer Daniel's prayer? (v23)
- **a)** After Daniel had finished praying
- **b)** As soon as Daniel began to pray
- **c)** A week later

THINK SPOT

When you write a letter or email, you sometimes have to wait a long time for a reply. But when you pray, God hears you straight away—and He's never slow at answering! Sometimes His answer will be 'No' or 'Wait'—but God always answers our prayers.

Like Daniel's prayer, Gabriel's answer is tricky to understand. Let's just look at the clear and important things in one verse...

READ
Daniel 9v25

- Just as God promised, His people would return to Israel and rebuild Jerusalem (v25).

    Check out your **Bible Timeline** to see when this happened. *This is the pic to look for.*

We'll read about this in the book of **Nehemiah** (Day 41).

- After Jerusalem was rebuilt, God's chosen King (*Anointed One*) would come (v25). That's <u>Jesus</u>.

    Find the birth of Jesus on your **Bible Timeline**.

PRAY

Jesus is going to come back to earth again. The world will end, and all of God's people will live with King Jesus in heaven. <u>Daniel</u> will be there! Will <u>you</u>? If you're a follower of Jesus, the answer is Yes!—so thank Him now. If you're not sure, check out 'God's Rescue Plan' after Day 30.

In the last few issues of XTB we've been reading John's book about Jesus.

READ John 20v31

Why did John write his book? Go forward one letter to fill in the missing words. (A=B, B=C, C=D etc)

So that you may _ _ _ _ _ _ _ _
A D K H D U D

that _ _ _ _ _ is the Christ (Messiah),
I D R T R

the _ _ _ of _ _ _,
R N M F N C

and that by believing you may have

_ _ _ _ in His name.
K H E D

John wants us to believe that Jesus is the **Christ** (Messiah). That means **God's chosen King**.

In his book, John tells us loads of amazing things that Jesus did and said.

They are all *signposts* pointing to who Jesus is. They help us understand more about Jesus.

Many of these signposts pointed to something amazing about Jesus —He came to earth so that He could **DIE** for us.

Here are some bits of John's book that show us that Jesus had to die...
John 2v18-22   John 7v33-34
John 12v1-8   John 12v32-33

Turn to the next page now!

READ
John 18v1-6

Jesus and his friends were walking at night when they met Judas with a bunch of soldiers. Judas was one of Jesus' disciples, His closest friends. Yet Judas handed Jesus over to be arrested by His enemies. What a traitor!

*Cross out all the **X**s then write out the remaining letters.*

XJXESXUXXSKXNEXWXXEVXERXX
YTXHIXXNGXXTHXATWAXXSG
OXINGTOXHAXXPPEXNTOXHIXM
JESUS_____

_____

_____ **(v4)**

Jesus **knew** that He would be arrested and would be killed. Jesus was surrounded by soldiers yet He was in control! He was so powerful, they fell to the ground!

READ
John 18v7-11

Jesus is so loving! Even when He was being arrested, He put others first.

• Jesus made sure that His disciples could get away (v8)

• He didn't want Peter to cut off the guard's ear (Luke 22v51 says that Jesus healed the guard!)

PRAY

Jesus let Himself be arrested because He knew He had to die. It was all part of God's amazing plan to rescue people. Say **thank you** to Jesus for giving up His life for people like you and me.

DAY 22 DON'T KEEP QUIET!

xtb · John 18v12-18

Oh no! Jesus has been arrested! What will happen to Him?

READ
John 18v12-14

Jesus was taken to Caiaphas, the very important Jewish high priest. He hated Jesus so much that he wanted to kill Him. In a few days' time we'll see if Caiaphas got his wish.

READ
John 18v15-18

Peter followed Jesus to find out what would happen to Him. A slave girl spoke to Peter. **Use verse 17 to fill in their speech bubbles.**

Yesterday we read how Peter **fought** for Jesus. Now he won't even say that he **knows** Jesus!

Are you a Christian?

You don't go to church do you???

THINK SPOT

How do **YOU** answer tricky questions like that? Are you honest or do you chicken out?

Peter had to learn a hard lesson. But later, he changed and wrote **1 Peter 3v15**. It's near the end of your Bible. *Read it and cross out all the wrong words in the box.*

Sometimes/always/never be prepared to answer/avoid anyone who asks you to give a reason for the hype/hoop/hope you have.

PRAY

That means Christians should be ready to tell people about Jesus. Ask God to give you the courage to let your friends know that you love Jesus.

DAY 23 TRIAL AND ERROR

After His arrest Jesus was put on trial. That means He was questioned by the Jewish leaders.

READ
John 18v19-24

Use the **flag code** to reveal what Annas questioned Jesus about.

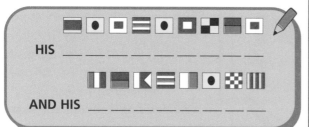

HIS _ _ _ _ _ _ _ _ _ _ _ _

AND HIS _ _ _ _ _ _ _ _ _ _ _

That doesn't sound too bad. But there were **3 things missing** from the trial...

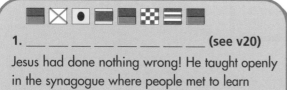

1. _ _ _ _ _ _ _ _ _ _ _ _ (see v20)
Jesus had done nothing wrong! He taught openly in the synagogue where people met to learn about God. He wasn't doing bad things secretly.

Flag Code

= A
= B
= C
= D
= E
= F
= G
= H
= I
= L
= N
= P
= R
= S
= T
= V
= W

2. _ _ _ _ _ _ _ _ _ _ _ _ _ (v21)
Loads of people could have spoken up for Jesus but were not given the chance. They would have told the priests the truth about Jesus.

3. _ _ _ _ _ _ _ _ _ _ _ _ (v22-24)
They had no evidence (proof) against Jesus, but wouldn't let Him go. Instead, they attacked Him and then sent Him to Caiaphas for another unfair trial.

PRAY

Jesus wasn't going to die for His own wrong—He hadn't done any wrong! Instead He would die for <u>our</u> wrong. He was the **only one** who could do that! What could you say to Him right now?

DAY 24 — CHICKEN!

Jesus was arrested and Peter followed Him. Let's find out what Jesus said to Peter earlier that evening...

READ
John 13v36-38

Jesus said that Peter would deny knowing Him. How many times (v38)?

Two days ago we read about Peter telling a girl that he didn't know Jesus.

READ
John 18v25-27

Jesus was right. Peter denied knowing Jesus three times. How do you think Peter felt when he realised what he'd done? *Circle the words that you think fit.*

ASHAMED   **NOT BOTHERED**

ANNOYED   **EMBARRASSED**

LIKE A TRAITOR   **HAPPY**

We all let Jesus down sometimes. In the next box, put a tick next to the things that you have done.

Kept quiet while people made fun of Jesus	
Said that you did "not much" on Sunday instead of mentioning church	
Felt too embarrassed to tell friends that you love Jesus	

We all make mistakes. But we can say sorry to God and He forgives us. Then we can try harder next time!

PRAY

Say sorry to God for the times you have let Him down. Ask Him to help you be braver so you talk to friends about Jesus.

DAY 25 PILATE PLOT

The Jewish leaders took Jesus to Pilate, the local Roman ruler. They hoped he would decide to put Jesus to death.

READ
John 18v28-30

These Jewish leaders were very careful in keeping <u>some</u> laws. They wouldn't enter the home of a non-Jewish person like Pilate during the Passover feast-time. But they weren't so bothered about <u>other</u> laws...

...like breaking all the rules about fair trials! And they didn't care that they were trying to send innocent Jesus to His death.

Despite their evil plan, it was **Jesus' plans** that were working out...

READ
John 18v31-32

xtb · John 18v28-32

Jesus had predicted all of this! Fill in the missing letter **Es** to reveal what Jesus said (it's in Matthew 20v17-19).

> **The Son of Man (Jesus) will be hand___d ov___r to the chi___f pri___sts and t___ach___rs of the law. Th___y will cond___mn him to d___ath, turn him ov___r to the G___ntiles (non-Jews) to be mock___d and whipp___d and crucifi___d.**

The Jewish leaders were not allowed to put anyone to death. But Pilate was a Roman and had the power to order Jesus to be killed. This was exactly what Jesus had said would happen! Somehow it was all part of God's plan!

PRAY

Dear God, I don't always understand why things happen. Thank You that I can still trust You because Your plans always work out!

DAY 26   CAPTURED KING

The Jewish leaders have taken Jesus to Pilate, the Roman governor. They want him to put Jesus to death.

READ
John 18v33-35

What did Pilate say to Jesus (v33)?

Are you the
_____?

The Jewish leaders would not accept Jesus as the **King** who had come to rescue them. And they wanted the Romans to think that He had come to fight them.

READ
John 18v36-37

Jesus said that He wasn't that kind of king. He hadn't come to fight against the Romans. He came to earth to tell people the **TRUTH**.

THINK SPOT

Do **YOU** believe the truth about Jesus? That He is the King of all God's people (Christians) and that He now rules as their King in heaven?

YES/NO _____

Use your **Bible Timeline** to check out when Jesus went back to heaven.
What's the special name for this?

A_____

READ
John 18v38-40

These people didn't believe that Jesus was the King who had come to rescue people from sin. Instead they wanted to kill Him! That is so tragic.

PRAY

Ask God to help you believe the truth about Jesus. Remember, He is the King in heaven who is in charge of you. So what difference will that make to the way you live?

J E T H G O S E P D E U S O I S I P S U
F N L C E R E F E O R J E N C T E D T R
F E D J O R O E S L U U S S

Jesus has been taken to Pilate, the local Roman ruler.

READ
John 19v1-3

How awful. Jesus was attacked and mocked. From the box at the top of the page, write out all the **RED** letters in the same order.

— — — — — —   — — — — — — — —
— — —   — — — — —

Jesus went through all of that so that He could die to take the punishment **we** deserve.

READ
John 19v4-7

Now write out all the **BLUE** letters in the next box.

— — — —   — — — — — — — —
— — — — — — — — — —   — — — — — —

They refused to believe that Jesus was God's Son. God had clearly said that Jesus was His Son. When?—check it out on your **Bible Timeline**.

READ
John 19v8-16

Now write out all the **GREEN** letters.

— — — —   — — — —   — — — — —
— — — — — — — —!

Jesus said that it was **GOD** who gave Pilate his power! Everything that was happening was part of God's plans!

PRAY

Thank God that He is in control of everything! Ask Him to help you really believe that Jesus is His Son who died to rescue you.

DAY 28 CROSS WORDS

Jesus had done nothing wrong, yet He was sentenced to death. But remember, it was all part of **God's plan to rescue people!**

READ
John 19v17-18

Jesus was nailed to a wooden cross and was left to die. Jesus went through that to rescue people like you and me! What incredible love!

READ
John 10v19-22

*What was written on the sign on Jesus' cross (v19)? Take the **first letter of each picture** to find out.*

The Jewish leaders were furious that Jesus was called their king. But Jesus **was** their King and not only their King, but the King of **everything**!

PRAY

King Jesus died on the cross to rescue people from their sin. If you really mean it, ask Jesus to be the King in charge of your whole life.

DAY 29 AMAZING LOVE

 John 19v23-27

READ
John 19v23-24

Jesus is dying on the cross, and these soldiers are gambling for His clothes! Casting lots means throwing dice to decide who would get the clothes.

READ
John 19v25-27

Jesus was in agony—but that didn't stop Him caring for His mother and making sure she would be looked after.

Flick back to **Psalm 22v18** and write it out.

Follow Jesus' example! Write down who you could be more loving towards. Then write down how you'll do it...

God helped King David to write these words many years before they came true! *Use your **Bible Timeline** to find out how many years before.*

It was <u>always</u> God's plan for Jesus to die on the cross to rescue us from sin!

PRAY

Jesus loves and cares for YOU too. Ask Him to help you be more loving to the people whose names you wrote down.

We're reading about the most important thing that's ever happened! Please turn your page on its side.

READ
John 19v28-30

What were Jesus' last words before He died (v30)?

It is _____

What three things were finished?

1. Old Testament prophecies

Write out the words of Psalm 69v21. They're about Jesus!

_____
_____
_____

1000 years before it happened, King David said that Jesus would be given vinegar to drink. It came true! The last prediction about Jesus' death had come true. It was time for Jesus to give up His life.

2. Jesus' suffering
Jesus suffered so much for people like you and me. He even took God's anger and punishment for us! All of that suffering was now finished.

3. Jesus' work
Jesus came to earth to rescue people from sin. By dying on the cross He took the punishment **we** deserve! So everyone who trusts Him, can have their sins forgiven by Him!

Turn to GOD'S RESCUE PLAN on the next page

GOD'S RESCUE PLAN

Why did God rescue us—and **who** is the Rescuer? *John 3v16* explains it.

For God loved the world so much...

This is the reason for the Rescue Plan. God's **everlasting love** for you and me. He wants us to know Him and to be His friends. But there's a problem. **SIN** gets in the way.

What is Sin?
We all like to be in charge of our own lives. We do what **we** want instead of what **God** wants. This is called Sin.

Sin gets in the way between us and God. It stops us from knowing Him and stops us from being His friends. The final result of sin is death. You can see why we need to be rescued!

...that He gave His only Son...

God sent **Jesus** to be our Rescuer—to save us from the problem of sin.

How did Jesus rescue us?
At the first Easter, when Jesus was about 33 years old, He was crucified. He was nailed to a cross and left to die.

As He died, all the sins of the world (all the wrongs people do) were put onto Jesus. He took all of our sin onto Himself, taking the punishment we deserve. He died in our place, as our Rescuer, so that we can be forgiven.

Did you know?
Jesus died on the cross as our Rescuer—but He didn't stay dead! After three days God brought Him back to life! Jesus is still alive today, ruling as our King.

...so that everyone who believes in Him may not die but have eternal life. (John 3v16)

When Jesus died He solved the problem of sin. That means that there is nothing to separate us from God any more. That's great news for you and me!

We can know God today as our Friend and King—and one day live in heaven with Him for ever.

Have YOU been rescued by Jesus? **Turn to the next page to find out more...**

AM I A CHRISTIAN?

Not sure if you're a Christian? Then check it out below...

Christians are people who have been rescued by Jesus and follow Him as their King.

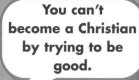

You can't become a Christian by trying to be good.

That's great news, since you can't be totally good all the time!

Being a Christian means accepting what Jesus did on the cross to rescue you. To do that, you will need to **ABCD**.

A **Admit** your sin—that you do, say and think wrong things. Tell God you are sorry. Ask Him to forgive you, and to help you to change. There will be some wrong things you have to stop doing.

B **Believe** that Jesus died for you, to take the punishment for your sin; that He came back to life, and that He is still alive today.

C **Consider** the cost of living like God's friend from now on, with Him in charge. It won't be easy. Ask God to help you do this.

D **Do** something about it! In the past you've gone your own way rather than God's way. Will you hand control of your life over to Him from now on? If you're ready to ABCD, then talk to God now. The prayer will help you.

A prayer

Dear God,
I have done and said and thought things that are wrong. I am really sorry. Please forgive me. Thank You for sending Jesus to die for me. From now on, please help me to live as one of Your friends, with You in charge.
                    Amen

Do you remember Jesus' promise?—'<u>everyone</u> who believes in Him shall not die but have eternal life.' *John 3v16*

Jesus welcomes <u>everyone</u> who comes to Him. If you have put your trust in Him, He has rescued you from your sins and will help you to live for Him. That's brilliant!

DAY 31 — SEEING IS BELIEVING

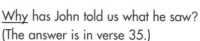
Tell me what happened as you walked past the bank.

I saw two men with stockings over their heads...

A **WITNESS** tells people what he or she saw to convince them about something. **John** is telling us what He saw when Jesus died...

READ
John 19v35

<u>Why</u> has John told us what he saw? (The answer is in verse 35.)

So that you _____

_____

What does John want us to believe?

READ
John 19v31-37

1. John wants us to believe that Jesus really died

If Jesus didn't really die, then He also wasn't raised back to life and He can't rescue us from sin. In verses 33-34 John tells that he saw Jesus' dead body himself. Jesus really **did** die for us!

---

2. John wants us to believe that Jesus is the Rescuer

In verses 36-37, John tells us two things that had been told about Jesus 100s of years before he was around. They both came true and prove that Jesus really is the One sent by God to **rescue** people.

THINK + PRAY

John was a **witness** to Jesus' death. Do you believe what he tells us about Jesus?

YES/NO _____

Ask God to help you believe that Jesus can **rescue** you from sin.

John 19v38-42

Jesus is dead, and His body must be moved before sunset.

READ
John 19v38-39

body	garden	**Jesus**
Joseph	killed	linen
Nicodemus	**night**	Pilate
secret	**spices**	tomb

*Use the **RED** words from the word pool to fill in the blanks.*

J_____ of Arimathea was a s_____ follower of Jesus. He asked P_____ if he could bury Jesus' b_____.

*Now use the **BLUE** words.*

Joseph was helped by N_____, who had once secretly visited J_____ in the n_____. He brought some s_____ with him.

READ
John 19v40-42

*Now fill in the **GREEN** words.*

They wrapped Jesus' body in l_____ and buried Him in a new t_____ in a g_____ near where He was k_____.

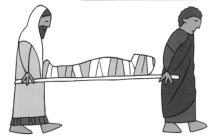

Not many people could have done that for Jesus.

What things can **YOU** do for Jesus? (Tell your friend about Jesus? Show your parents more respect?)

THINK SPOT

_____

_____

_____

PRAY

Ask God to help you do those things for Jesus. And make sure you do them!

DAY 33 TOMB RAIDERS?

Jesus has died and been buried. But that's not the end of the story!

READ
John 20v1-2

Who spotted the empty tomb?

M_____   M_____

She told Peter and John that someone had stolen Jesus' body!

Did you know?

The 'disciple Jesus loved' in verse 2 is **John** who is writing this story!

READ
John 20v3-8

Who got to the tomb first (v4)?

J_____

Who was first to go inside (v6)?

S_____   P_____

They saw that Jesus' body was gone! And His grave clothes were neatly folded up, so it can't have been robbers!

READ
John 20v9

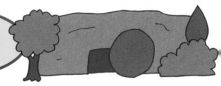

The Scriptures (the oldest part of the Bible) said that Jesus would come back to life again. Jesus had said so too. But the disciples had not understood it.

 THINK SPOT
Do you sometimes find it hard to understand the Bible? Maybe you find some of it hard to **believe**?

What did John do when he saw Jesus' body missing from the tomb?

He s_____ and b_____ (v8)

PRAY
*Ask God to help you **understand** what He's saying to you in the Bible. And to **believe** what the Bible says.*

DAY 34 BIG SURPRISE!

Mary, Peter and John had discovered that Jesus' body was no longer in His tomb! Mary was upset because she thought that robbers had stolen it.

READ
John 20v10-13

Mary didn't realise that the two men were angels. And she was about to get an even bigger surprise...

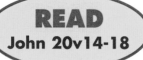
READ
John 20v14-18

Who was standing behind Mary (v14)?

John	
Jesus	

Who did Mary think He was (v15)?

the plumber	☐
the electrician	☐
the gardener	☐

But as soon as Jesus said her name, Mary realised who it was. She was so happy! Jesus was alive!!!

Jesus told Mary to tell the disciples that He would soon be going back to heaven.

*Grab your **Bible Timeline** and look at the section about the life of Jesus. Mark '**X**' on the line where you think Mary met the risen Jesus.*

What did Mary do (v18)?

kept her mouth shut	☐
told only one person	☐
told the disciples that Jesus was alive	☐

Mary had been **sad**.
But now she was so-o-o **happy** that Jesus was alive!

THINK + PRAY

Are <u>you</u> excited that Jesus is alive? It means He can help you now and, one day, take you to live for ever in heaven. Ask God to help you be excited about Jesus.

READ
John 20v19-20

The disciples were meeting secretly in a locked room. Suddenly Jesus appeared in the middle of them! They were so happy that Jesus was alive!

Crack the flag code to reveal what Jesus said to them (v20).

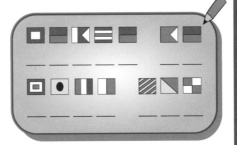

That meant **hello** in those days. But Jesus really can bring us **PEACE**. He can give us peace with God, and rescue us from sin. (To find out how, turn to **GOD'S RESCUE PLAN** on the page after Day 30.)

READ
John 20v21-23

Flag Code

= A
= B
= C
= D
= E
= F
= G
= H
= I
= N
= O
= P
= R
= S
= T
= U
= W
= Y

What else did Jesus say (v21)?

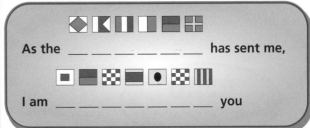

As the _ _ _ _ _ _ _ _ has sent me,

I am _ _ _ _ _ _ _ _ you

Everyone who has been rescued by Jesus has a job to do. They must tell others about Jesus and how He can forgive their sins. And Jesus gives them the Holy Spirit to help them do it!

PRAY

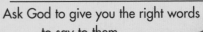

Write down the name of someone you could talk to about Jesus.

_____

Ask God to give you the right words to say to them.

DAY 36 BELIEVE IT OR NOT?

xtb John 20v24-31

Thomas didn't see Jesus meet the other disciples. Would he believe what they said?

READ
John 20v24-29

At first, did Thomas believe them? **Yes / No**

In the end, what did Thomas say? *Go forward one letter to find out (A=B, B=C, C=D, Z=A etc).*

L X   K N Q C

Z M C   L X

___ ___ ___!
F N C

At last, Thomas believed that Jesus was God's Son—but only because he <u>saw</u> Him.

How can I believe Jesus is God's Son alive forever? I can't see Him!

Jesus said people like us <u>can</u> believe, even if we haven't seen Him. (It's in verse 29.)

We too can hear what the disciples said, because it's written in the New Testament part of our Bibles.

Jesus' followers wrote down what they had seen Jesus do. Did you know most of them were killed for this?

Are you like Thomas? Or do you believe what they've said?

READ
John 20v30-31

Why did John write about the amazing things Jesus did?

So <u>you</u> believe that

___ ___ ___ ___ ___   ___ ___
I D R T R   H R

___ ___ ___   ___ ___ ___
S G D   R N M

___ ___   ___ ___ ___
N E   F N C

If you're not sure about believing that Jesus is <u>your</u> Lord and God, turn to **AM I A CHRISTIAN** on the page before Day 31.

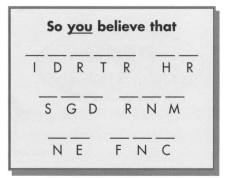

PRAY Thank God for giving us the true story of Jesus, written by His followers. Ask Him to help you read and believe it.

xtb John 21v1-14

Jesus died, but God raised Him back to life! Wonderful! But what should the disciples do now?

READ
John 21v1-3

Peter suggested that they all go fishing. How many fish did they catch (v3)?

READ
John 21v4-14

Who was waiting for them on the shore (v4)?

Who helped them to catch loads of fish?

Did you know this had happened before? (It's in Luke 5v1-11.) It was when Jesus first met some of His disciples. They were going to follow Jesus and do a new job...

From now on you will catch men.

Jesus didn't mean they would catch people in a huge net! He meant the disciples would tell people about Jesus and help them follow Him too.

But what were they trying to catch now? (v3)   **People / Fish**

The disciples were happy that Jesus was alive. But now they wanted to go back to normal life—catching fish.

But Jesus didn't agree!

Why did Jesus help them catch so many fish? (*Find two correct answers.*)
- because they were very hungry.
- to remind them to go on living their new lives, doing their new job.
- so they could become rich, famous fishermen.
- to show that they couldn't live without His help.

Jesus' resurrection means...

...He is God's King, so we should live to serve Him.

...He can save everyone from sin, so we should tell people about Him.

PRAY Has your life changed to do these things? Or are you still living your normal old life? Remember, because Jesus is alive He can help you. Ask God for help to live for Jesus and never give up.

DAY 38 FEED MY SHEEP

 John 21v15-17

Do you remember the disciple called **Peter**? (He's also known as *Simon Peter* and *Simon*.) He's the one who pretended that he didn't know Jesus (flick back to Day 24 for a reminder).

READ
John 21v15-17

What did Jesus ask Peter? Cross out the Xs and write down what's left.

XDXXOXXYXXOXXUXX
LXXOXXVEXXXMXEX?

D_____?

How did Peter answer?

YES/NO _____

 How many times had Peter denied knowing Jesus? (see Mark 14v72)

 How many times did Jesus ask Peter if he loved Him?

Jesus was showing Peter that he **forgave** him! We all mess up and let Jesus down sometimes. But we can say sorry to Jesus and He will forgive us! Then we can get back to living in a way that pleases Jesus.

What did Jesus tell Peter to do (v17)? Cross out the Xs again!

XFXEXEXXXDXMXXY
XSHXXXXEXEXXPXX

F_____

Jesus gave Peter the special job of looking after His sheep—that means followers of Jesus.

PRAY *Thank You Jesus that You love Your followers and forgive them when they let You down. Please help me to live to serve You. Amen*

READ
John 21v18-19

Complete what Jesus said to Peter. Find the missing words in the wordsearch (below).

"When you are **o**_____, you will **s**_____ out your **h**_____ and someone will dress you and **l**_____ you where you don't want to go". Jesus said this to show **P**_____ that he would **d**_____ for following Jesus and would bring **g**_____ to God. Then Jesus said "**F**_____ me".

```
N S C J P U O D F
C U E T W B V I X
F O L L O W G E S
Y L D F E B E C T
H E F H P E T E R
E A V S U S E J E
S D E G L O R Y T
M K G A Z L D R C
N D L Q S D N A H
```

Peter became a great leader, telling thousands of people about Jesus! But he was killed for it. Following Jesus isn't easy! People will tease you and hassle you. In some countries, people are even killed for following Jesus.

Check out on your **Bible Timeline** what will happen to <u>all</u> Christians in the end.

READ
John 21v20-24

Peter asked Jesus what would happen to John. Jesus told him not to worry about John, but to concentrate on serving God.

Don't get too wrapped up in what other people do—make sure that YOU are living God's way!

PRAY

Dear God, please help me to serve You, even if I get hassle for it. Help Christians today who could be killed. Thank You that we can live for ever in heaven with You.

DAY 40 BOOK ENDS

You've reached the end of John's book about Jesus. Well done! John has told us so many things that Jesus did and said. Find some of them by looking up the verses and then drawing lines to match them with the right description.

| John 2v7-11 |
| John 3v16 |
| John 6v8-13 |
| John 19v17-18 |

Jesus said that people who trust in Him will have eternal life.

Jesus died on the cross to rescue people from sin.

Jesus turned water into wine.

Jesus fed thousands of people with a tiny amount of food.

All these things are **signposts**. They point us to the truth that Jesus is the one who God sent to **rescue** people from sin.

READ
John 21v25

Jesus did so many amazing things! Far more than John could write about or we could ever have the time to read!

Do you remember why John wrote this book? (The clue is in **John 20v31**.)

So that you **b**_____ that Jesus is the **C**_____ the **S**_____ of **G**_____, and that by believing you may have **l**_____ in his name.

John wants us to **believe** that Jesus is the Christ – the King who can rescue us from sin, so we can live with Him as King of our lives!

THINK + PRAY

Do **you** believe that Jesus is the great Rescuer? Is He the King in charge of your life? Tell God your answers. And please talk to a parent or older Christian about your answers. Go on, don't be shy!

DAY 41 HISTORY HOP

Ahem! Attention please! Time for a quick pogo through Bible history...

*Find each person or event on your **Bible Timeline** as you read about them.*

• Abraham

God promised to give Abraham a HUGE family. They were called the Israelites.

• Moses

The Israelites were <u>slaves</u> in Egypt. But God rescued them (with Moses as their leader) and gave them the land of Canaan to live in.

• Judges

For 400 years the Israelites had judges to lead them. But then they demanded a king of their own (even though <u>God</u> was their Real King!).

• Kings

1. <u>Saul</u> was the first king of Israel —but he turned away from God.
2. <u>David</u> was the best king they ever had. He loved God.
3. When David's son <u>Solomon</u> became king, he built a great temple for God in Jerusalem. But later, Solomon turned away from God and worshipped pretend gods instead.

• Exile

God warned His people that if they turned away from Him they would be turned out of their country. (This is called exile.) But they didn't listen! So God allowed most of the Israelites to be captured by the Assyrians, and sent to live in far off countries.

• Daniel

The rest of the Israelites were captured by King Nebuchadnezzar of Babylon. They included Daniel and his friends S,M&A. Jerusalem was destroyed and the temple torn down.

Turn to the next page to find out more.

DAY 41 HISTORY = HIS STORY
CONTINUED

On Day 19, we saw Daniel cry out to God to keep His promise to bring His people back to Jerusalem.

God answered Daniel's prayer. The first group of Israelites came back to Jerusalem a few years later. We're going to dip into the book of Ezra to see what they said about themselves.

READ
Ezra 5v11-16

Draw lines to match each verse with what happened.
(The first is started for you.)

verse 11

verse 12

verse 13

verse 16

A The exile to Babylon was God's punishment because His people had turned away from Him.

B The Israelites had been rebuilding the temple ever since they returned to Jerusalem. But it wasn't finished yet.

C God's temple had been built by Solomon and destroyed by King Neb. Now the Israelites were rebuilding it.

D King Cyrus of Persia wasn't one of God's people. But God caused Cyrus to send the Israelites back to Jerusalem to rebuild the temple. (Ezra 1v1)

Now copy all the red letters (in order, from both pages) to see something very important about God.

G _ _ _ ' _ _ _ _ _ _

a _ _ _ _ _ _

_ _ _ _ _ t _ _ _ _

PRAY

God warned His people what would happen if they turned away from Him. But they didn't listen, so He sent them into exile. He also promised to bring them back 70 years later, and He did. God's words <u>always</u> come true! Ask God to help you believe and obey His words as you read them in the Bible.

DAY 42 BAD NEWS

Today we're going to start the book of Nehemiah. As we saw yesterday, God had made King Cyrus of Persia send some of the Israelites back to Jerusalem to rebuild the temple.

Many years later some Israelites still lived in Persia. One of them was **Nehemiah**. He was a trusted servant of the king.

Nehemiah was waiting for his brother to come back from Jerusalem. He would have news of how the Israelites (Jews) who lived there were getting on...

READ
Nehemiah 1v1-4

What was the news? (v3)

- The **people** were a) very happy
  b) in trouble

- The city **walls** were a) broken down
  b) being built

- The city **gates** were a) safely locked
  b) burnt

Answers: b,a,b

Draw Nehemiah's face when he heard this terrible news.

Nehemiah was terribly upset—so he turned to God in prayer. *We'll read his prayer tomorrow...*

THINK + PRAY

God's people in Jerusalem were in great trouble, so Nehemiah <u>prayed</u> for them. Today there are some countries where God's people (Christians) are treated very badly because they love Jesus. Pray for those Christians now. Ask God to be with them, and help them to stand up for Him, even when that's very hard.
If you can, ask an older Christian to help you to find out more about people who suffer for being followers of Jesus.

DAY 43 THE WAY TO PRAY

 Nehemiah 1v4-11

What's the first thing you do when you hear bad news?

Nehemiah had just heard that the Israelites in Jerusalem were in trouble, and that the city itself was in a terrible state. Nehemiah was so upset that he **wept** about it. But he also **prayed**...

READ
Nehemiah 1v4-11

Prayer Code

= A
= C
= D
= E
= F
= G
= H
= I
= L
= M
= N
= O
= P
= R
= S
= T

When <u>Nehemiah</u> prayed...

A—Verse 5

...he said how __ __ __ __ __ God is. And how good He is to all who love Him.

B—Verses 6 & 7

...he __ __ __ __ __ __ __ __ __ __ __ that he and all the Israelites had sinned terribly against God.

C—Verses 8 & 9

...he remembered God's

__ __ __ __ __ __ __ __ to scatter them if they disobeyed and bring them back if they turned back to God.

D—Verse 11

...he pleaded for God's __ __ __ __ with a plan to ask the king a big favour.

When <u>you</u> pray...

Use the same words to fill in the gaps.

A—do you show respect and praise to our **g**_____ God?

B—do you **c**_____ the wrong things you've done?

C—do you thank God for His **p**_____ to forgive people who turn to Him?

D—do you ask for God's **h**_____ in everything you do?

PRAY Talk to God now, using these four steps (A, B, C, D).

L—O—N—G Prayer

It was the Jewish month of **Kislev** when Nehemiah heard the bad news about Jerusalem and its people (Nehemiah 1v1).

As a result he started to pray:
- He praised his **great** God.
- He **confessed** that he and the Israelites had sinned.
- He remembered God's **promise**.
- He prayed for God's **help** when he asked the king for a favour.

Four months later, in the Jewish month of **Nisan**, Nehemiah was still praying!

Find all the <u>blue words</u> in the wordsearch.

Some are backwards!

P	D	E	S	S	E	F	N	O	C
R	A	Y	A	K	I	S	L	E	V
P	L	E	H	T	G	R	E	A	T
N	I	S	A	N	A	L	L	T	I
E	S	I	M	O	R	P	M	E	S

THINK SPOT
If you're worried about something, don't just pray about it once! Keep praying, until you know what God's answer is.

SHORT Prayer

Nehemiah was a trusted servant, who served the king's wine. One day, God answered Nehemiah's prayers by giving him a chance to speak to the king...

READ
Nehemiah 2v1-6

Why was the king surprised? (v1)

> Nehemiah looked so **s**_____

When Nehemiah told the king about Jerusalem, the king asked what he wanted. What did Nehemiah do? (v4)

> He **p**_____

THINK SPOT
Sometimes there isn't time for a l-o-n-g prayer. A quick prayer is fine—God already knows what you need!

God's answer this time was very quick. The king agreed that Nehemiah could go back to Jerusalem to rebuild it (v6).

Copy the <u>leftover letters</u> from the wordsearch (in order) to see something the Bible says about prayer.

— — — — — — — —

— — — — —

1 Thessalonians 5v17

PRAY
You can pray anytime, anywhere, about anything! What do you want to talk to God about right now?

Today we'll meet loads of people with odd names! But are they good guys or bad guys? *We'll find out...*

Nehemiah has just asked the king of Persia to let him go and rebuild Jerusalem. But it's a l-o-n-g way (two months travel!) and he'll need help...

READ
Nehemiah 2v6-10

Did King Artaxerxes agree that Nehemiah could go? (v6)

→ **Yes**—*give the king a happy face.*

→ **No**—*give the king an angry face.*

The king also wrote letters to make sure that Nehemiah could travel safely, and would have the wood he needed to build with. (v7-8)

Draw happy faces for the governors of West Euphrates and Asaph the forest keeper.

How did Sanballat and Tobiah feel when they heard Nehemiah's plans? (v10)

→ **Pleased**—*give them happy faces.*

→ **Upset**—*give them angry faces.*

King Artaxerxes of Persia

Governors of West Euphrates

Asaph, keeper of royal forests

Sanballat the Horonite

Tobiah the Ammonite

Nehemiah got <u>loads</u> of help from the king. He even sent soldiers to keep Nehemiah safe! (v9) *Verse 8 tells us why...*

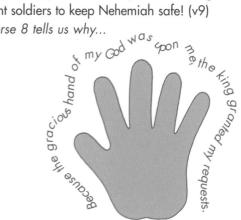

Because the gracious hand of my God was upon me, the king granted my requests.

This doesn't mean that Nehemiah had a huge hand on his head! It means that God was <u>with</u> Nehemiah, showing him great kindness.

THINK + PRAY Nehemiah had great plans for Jerusalem— but they only worked out because God was with him. Do you have plans to serve God? If they are <u>His</u> plans too, He will help you. Talk to Him about them now.

As you read today's verses, draw lines to match the speech and thought bubbles with the right people.

READ
Nehemiah 2v11-20

Nehemiah

I didn't tell anyone what God had inspired me to do. (v12)

I told them how God had been kind to me. (v18)

Let us start rebuilding. (v18)

What is this you are doing? (v19)

The God of heaven will give us success. (v20)

Israelites

Sanballat & Tobiah

How quickly did the people agree to start rebuilding? (v18)

a) Straight away
b) A few weeks later
c) Two years later

 THINK SPOT

When **you** get the chance to do something for God, do you do it as soon as possible?

What did Sanballat and Tobiah do? (v19)

a) Helped the Israelites
b) Laughed at the Israelites
c) Paid the Israelites

THINK + PRAY

When we do what God wants us to do, we will sometimes get laughed at—like these Israelites. But Nehemiah wasn't put off. Why not? (v20)

_____ will give us success.

God wants Christians to do His work and will help us if we ask Him. Don't be put off by people who tease you. Ask God to help you do what He wants.

Did you notice that everything Nehemiah thought or said was about **God**? He knew that <u>God</u> had chosen him to rebuild Jerusalem, and that only <u>God</u> could help them to do it.

Chapter 3 lists all the people who rebuilt the walls, and which bits they built. *Check out the <u>blue verse numbers</u> to find the names of the city gates they rebuilt.*

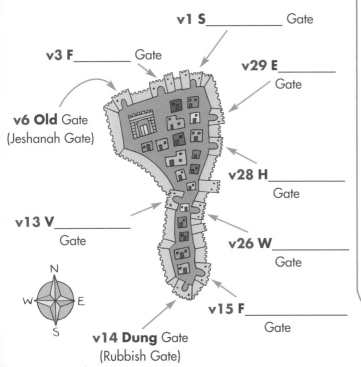

v1 S_____ Gate

v3 F_____ Gate

v6 Old Gate (Jeshanah Gate)

v29 E_____ Gate

v28 H_____ Gate

v13 V_____ Gate

v26 W_____ Gate

v15 F_____ Gate

v14 Dung Gate (Rubbish Gate)

Everyone got involved—except for a few lazy nobles! (v5) *Cross out every **X,Y**&**Z** to see who helped.*

XPRYIEZSXTSY (v1)

ZZSYONXSZ (v3)

ZGOYLDZSMXITYHSZ (v8)

YPERXXFUZME - MZAKYERXSZ (v8)

YDXAUXGHTXERYSZ (v12)

ZSEYRVXANYTSX (v26)

YYMEXRCZHANYTSZZ (v32)

THINK + PRAY

Everyone can serve God. Don't let anyone tell you that you're too young or not important or gifted enough. If you tell God you want to serve Him, then He will give you ways to do it! If that's what you want to do, tell Him so now.

DAY 48 PRAYER AND ACTION

Sally is being teased for being a Christian. What should she do?
a) Pray
b) Ask an older Christian for help
c) _____

Use the **word wall** to fill in the gaps below.

The Israelites were being laughed at by their enemies (v1-3).

What can those f_____ Jews do with all that rubble?

Even a **f**_____ could knock that wall down!

But when Nehemiah heard this he **p**_____ about it, and the Israelites kept rebuilding the wall until it reached **h**_____ its full height (v4-6).

Them their enemies plotted to attack Jerusalem!

But the Israelites **p**_____ to God, and also put men on **g**_____ day and night (v7-9).

Some of the Israelites were afraid—but Nehemiah told them to remember how <u>great</u> God is…

READ
Nehemiah 4v14-20

Don't be **a**_____.
Remember the **L**_____.
F_____ for your families.

Nehemiah kept a trumpeter with him, to call the Israelites to fight if needed.

Wherever you hear the **t**_____, join us there.
Our **G**_____ will fight for us.

Nehemiah and the Israelites **prayed** a lot—and **did** a lot too! **Prayer _and_ action**. They knew they could only build the wall and beat their enemies if their great God helped them.

PRAY

When you have a problem, do you do the same? **Pray _and_ do** something! Talk to God about anything that's bothering you.

WORD WALL: afraid | guard | half | LORD | prayed | Fight | fox | prayed | feeble | trumpet | God

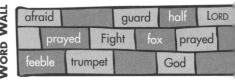

DAY 49 REBUILDING

What has Nehemiah been rebuilding?

Did you put 'the walls of Jerusalem'? If so, you're right. But they're not the only thing that needs rebuilding!

Take the first letter of each pic to see what else Nehemiah needed to rebuild.

__ __ __ __ ' __ __ __ __ __ __

The Israelites (Jews) in Jerusalem were <u>God's</u> people. But they weren't living the way <u>God</u> wanted them to!

The __ __ __ __ rulers were taking advantage of the rest.

The __ __ __ __ people had to sell their land and homes to these rulers. Some even sold their children as slaves!

Nehemiah was very angry with the rich rulers...

READ Nehemiah 5v9

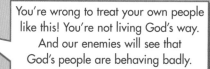

> You're wrong to treat your own people like this! You're not living God's way. And our enemies will see that God's people are behaving badly.

These were <u>God's</u> people. They should be living the way <u>God</u> wanted them to.

Nehemiah <u>did</u> live God's way...

READ Nehemiah 5v14-19

This chapter gives us two top reasons for living God's way:

1. Because other people see how we live. (v9)
(*When we do wrong, we dishonour God. Other people notice, and think Christianity is not worth much.*)

2. Because we love and respect God. (v15)
(*If we love God, we will want to please Him.*)

THINK + PRAY

Living God's way includes showing kindness to the poor. How can <u>you</u> do this? (*eg: give some of your pocket money to charity*). Ask God to show you who you can help. And how. Then do it!

DAY 50 A TRIO OF PLOTS

Nehemiah's enemies were still trying to stop him from rebuilding the walls...

PLOT ONE (v1-4)

> Come and meet us on the plain of Ono.

But Ono was a day's journey away, and Nehemiah knew the work would stop while he was gone.

So he said 'Oh No' to Ono!

PLOT TWO (v5-9)

Next, Sanballat sent an unsealed letter (which meant everyone could read the lies written in it).

READ
Nehemiah 6v5-9

> You are planning to revolt against the king of Persia and make yourself king.

But it wasn't true.
Sanballat was making it all up!

What was Sanballat trying to do? (v9)

F_____ **them.**

But what did Nehemiah do? (v9)

He p_____.

PLOT THREE (v10-14)

This time Nehemiah's enemies got a pretend prophet to give him a message from God.

> Run and hide in the temple. Your life is in danger!

But Nehemiah knew this man was lying. He wouldn't run away, because he had to finish the job God had given him.

THE RESULT (v15-16)

What was the result of all these plots?

READ
Nehemiah 6v15-16

Despite everything that their enemies tried, the wall was finished in only _____ days! (v15)

What did everyone realise? (v16)

The work had been done with

_____

PRAY

Nehemiah's powerful enemies couldn't stop the walls being finished, because <u>God</u> was helping His people. Thank God that nothing and no one can stop His plans.

DAY 51 LISTEN & LEARN

xtb Nehemiah 8v1-8

What has Nehemiah been rebuilding?

The walls were finished. But the people weren't!

They needed to know more about God and how He wanted them to live. That meant listening to God's Word...

READ
Nehemiah 8v1-8

Who read God's Word to the people? (v2)
- **a)** Ebenezer the prophet
- **b)** Ezra the priest
- **c)** Edith the professor

What did the people do? (v3)
- **a)** Listened for a while
- **b)** Listened on their headphones
- **c)** Listened attentively

What did the people say? (v6)

A_____! A_____!

Did you know?

Amen means 'so be it' or 'I agree'. We often say it at the end of a prayer to show that we agree with what was said.

Have you noticed that God's Word (the Bible) can sometimes be hard to understand? If the Israelites were going to rebuild their lives—to live as <u>God's</u> people—they needed help to understand what God was saying to them. Who helped them? (v7)

The L_____

The Levites were a group of Israelites who served God in His temple.

PRAY

Who helps <u>you</u> understand the Bible?

_____

Thank God for them, and ask Him to help them to teach His Word clearly so that you and many others can know God.

DAY 52 REMEMBER REMEMBER

The Israelites had spent <u>all</u> morning listening to God's Word. How do you think they felt?

tired? *sad?*

bored? *happy?*

READ
Nehemiah 8v9-12

Read the verses to find out.

The people were <u>crying</u> as they heard God's Law, because they knew they hadn't kept it. They hadn't lived the way God wanted them to.

But what did Nehemiah tell them? (v10)

> The j_____ of the L_____
> will make you strong.

Nehemiah sent the people home to <u>celebrate</u> all that God had done for them. But the next day they came back to hear more from God's Word...

READ
Nehemiah 8v13-18

Ummm... Why did they have to live in shelters???

XTB XPLANATION

The Festival of Shelters (or Booths or Tabernacles) was meant to be held every year. It reminded the Israelites of the time when God had rescued them from Egypt. As they travelled to the new land God had promised them, with <u>Moses</u> as their leader, they lived in temporary shelters or tents. After <u>Joshua</u> led them into Canaan, they settled into permanent homes. *Find **Moses** and **Joshua** on your **Bible Timeline**.*

How many of the people celebrated the Festival of Shelters? (v17) **None / Some / All**

THINK + PRAY

It's really important to remember the great things God has done for us. That's why we celebrate Christmas and Easter. What can <u>you</u> do this week to remind you of something God has done for you?

_____

Ask God to help you.

DAY 53 SO-O-O SORRY

READ
Nehemiah 9v1

What were the Israelites wearing?
a) Sailcloth
b) Sackcloth
c) Cheesecloth

What did they put on their heads?
a) Shampoo
b) Hats
c) Dust

Did you know?

Sackcloth and dust were a way of showing sadness and sorrow. The Israelites were showing how sorry they were for disobeying God's laws.

READ
Nehemiah 9v2-6

You **alone** are the LORD.
You made the **heavens**.
You made all the **stars**.
You made the **earth** and **seas** and everything in them.
You give life to **everything**.

Find all of the <u>blue words</u> in the wordsearch.

C	S	R	A	T	S	S	E	A	S
O	N	F	E	S	A	L	O	N	E
G	N	I	H	T	Y	R	E	V	E
H	T	R	A	E	S	W	O	R	S
H	E	A	V	E	N	S	H	I	P

Copy the <u>leftover letters</u> (in order) to spell two new words.

C _ _ _ _ _ _
W _ _ _ _ _ _

The people spent a quarter of the day (at least three hours!) praying. They were **confessing** (saying <u>sorry</u> to God) and **worshipping** (telling God how <u>great</u> He is).

PRAY

Use the same pattern for <u>your</u> prayers today. Start by telling God how **sorry** you are for letting Him down. Then tell Him how **great** He is (think of at least three reasons!).

DAY 54 YOU, YOU, YOU

As you read the next part of the Israelites' prayer to God, put a **tick** in the box every time you read '**You**'.

This means **God**.

READ
Nehemiah 9v7-15

God chose **Abram** to be the start of the Israelite nation. What new name did God give to Abram? (v7)

A_____

Abraham means 'father of many'. God promised to give Abraham a HUGE family—and He did! They were the Israelites. *Find **Abraham** on your **Bible Timeline**.*

The <u>same</u> word fits into all the gaps below. Work out what the missing word is, and write it in the spaces.

v7-8 _____ promised to give Abraham's family a land of their own. _____ kept His promise.

v9-10 Abraham's family (the Israelites) became slaves in Egypt. _____ sent miracles (the ten plagues) to rescue them.

v11-12 _____ made a dry path through the Red Sea to save His people from the Egyptian army.

v13-14 At Mount Sinai, _____ gave the Israelites laws to show them how to live as <u>His</u> people.

v15 As they travelled across the desert to their new land, _____ gave His people food and water.

Although this is the history of the Israelites—it's really all about <u>God</u>! **History = His Story**.

Can you write a history of <u>your</u> life, showing how God has helped you? It might start like this:

> *God gave me a home to live in and people to love me…*

Now thank God for these things.

DAY 55 BUT, BUT, BUT

Yesterday's reading was all 'You, you, you' as the Israelites listed the great things God had done for them.
But today's reading starts with a very sad word: **But...**

READ
Nehemiah 9v16-21

But they...
God had done <u>so</u> much for His people. They should have loved and obeyed Him. But they didn't!

What were the Israelites like? (v16-17)
(*Different Bible versions use slightly different words. <u>Underline</u> the words <u>your</u> Bible uses.*)

stubborn   *forgot the miracles*   *stiff-necked*   *proud*

arrogant   *refused to listen*   *failed to remember*

But God...
Even though the Israelites turned away from God, He was still loving and good.
(Circle) the words that describe God. (v17)

great love   *kind*   *slow to be angry*

forgiving   *compassionate*   *loving*   *mercy*

gracious   *slow to anger*   *abounding in love*

But today...
These things happened thousands of years ago. But God doesn't change! He is still loving, kind and forgiving today.

THINK + PRAY
Sometimes you and I are like those Israelites. We turn away from God and don't keep His commands. But God is loving and forgiving. That's why He sent Jesus, so that we can be forgiven for our wrongs, and be friends with God again. Say sorry to God for anything you have done today that let Him down. Thank Him for sending Jesus so that you can be forgiven.

DAY 56 END TO END

The prayer in chapter 9 is a short history of the Israelites:

Use your **Bible Timeline** to fill in the gaps.

- It starts with God's promises to **A**_____
- The Israelites settled in Egypt at the time of **J**_____
- When they became slaves, God chose **M**_____ to rescue His people from Egypt.
- After crossing the desert, it was **J**_____ who led the Israelites into the promised land of Canaan.
- But the people kept turning away from God, so He allowed their enemies to attack them. When the people cried out to God for help, He chose Judges to rescue them. **G**_____ was one of those Judges.
- Later, the people demanded a king—even though <u>God</u> was their Real King. Their first king was **S**_____ —but he turned away from God.
- **D**_____ was the best king of all. He loved God.
- When David's son **S**_____ became king, he built a great temple for God. But later, he turned away from God, and his kingdom became divided.
- The Israelites continued to disobey God's laws. So He allowed them to be captured by the Assyrians and the Babylonians. Some of them came back to Jerusalem at the time of **N**_____.

In the last few days, we've seen how God was always **faithful** to the Israelites. (He always kept His promises.) But they were **faithless**. (They didn't keep theirs!)
This is summed up in these verses:

READ
Nehemiah 9v33-37

PRAY

God is <u>always</u> faithful! **Read v33 again**. Nothing you or I do can make God break His promises! He always does what is right and good. How does that make you feel? Talk to Him about it now.

AN AGREEMENT WITH GOD

xtb — Nehemiah 9v38–10v39

> Yesterday, we learnt that nothing we do can make God break His promises?

🚩🚩🔲

> He is always loving and faithful?

🚩🚩🔲

> Does that mean it doesn't matter what I do or how I live?

🏁🔺 __ __ !

The Israelites knew that God was loving and faithful. But this didn't mean they could just live as they pleased!

READ
Nehemiah 9v38

What did the Israelites make?
- **a)** Excuses
- **b)** An agreement
- **c)** A cake

This written agreement was between the Israelites and God...

READ
Nehemiah 10v28-29

Flag Code

- 🏴 = A
- ▬ = D
- ▬ = E
- ||| = G
- ▢ = K
- ◼ = L
- ◣ = N
- ◥ = O
- ▭ = P
- ⊞ = R
- ▭ = S
- ⊠ = V
- ▢ = W
- 🟨 = Y

What were the Israelites agreeing to do? (v29)

__ __ __ __ __ , __ __ __ __ __

The people promised to live the way God wanted them to, and look after His temple. (v30-39)

Who made this agreement? (v28)

__ __ __ __ __ __ __ __

The priests, leaders, servants... ...and all the sons and daughters who were old enough to understand.

Are <u>you</u> ready to make this kind of agreement with God? Think carefully about it, and read the words below. Then if you want to, **sign** your name at the bottom.
(This is an important agreement, so don't worry if you're not ready. Ask God to help you to keep thinking about it until you are.)

AGREEMENT
Dear God, thank You that You are always loving and faithful. Thank You for the Bible that shows me how You want me to live. I commit myself to living Your way and keeping Your laws. Please help me to do this.
Signed:

NEW WALLS

My mum and dad live in Chester, which has an old Roman wall round it. I've walked round the walls of Chester loads of times—but not how Nehemiah did!

Nehemiah called together a huge crowd of singers and musicians.

They split into two large choirs...

...both standing on top of the new walls.

Ezra's group went **right**.

Nehemiah's went **left**.

They walked all round the walls—singing praise and thanks to God.

Then they met up again at God's temple.

READ
Nehemiah
12v40-43

Based on Nehemiah 12v27-40

Great s_____ (v43)
• The people gave many sacrifices (gifts) to God.

Great j_____ (v43)
• The people were full of joy—given to them by God.

Great noise!
• Where could the celebrations be heard? (v43).

At the beginning of Nehemiah's book, he was very sad because Jerusalem was in ruins. Now the city was rebuilt, with strong walls to protect it. No wonder the people were so full of joy!

THINK + PRAY
The people marched and sang to show their thanks to God. How can <u>you</u> thank God today? (*Try and pick something you don't usually do—like singing, making something, having a celebration...*)

Nehemiah had been rebuilding two things—the **walls** and the **people**. The walls were finished. They were **strong** and **safe**. But what about the people???

On Day 57 we saw that the people made an **agreement** with God. *Cross out the Xs to see what they agreed to do.*

- Not to **XMXXARXRYX** people who didn't **follow** God. (10v30)

- Not to buy or sell on God's **XREXST XXDAXY** (the **Sabbath**). (10v31)

- Give money and gifts for God's **XXTEXMPXXLEX**. (10v32-39)

BUT the people did **XXNXOXXTX** keep their **promises**!

Read Nehemiah 13v10-11

- They stopped **giving** to the temple.

Read Nehemiah 13v15-16

- They were **buying** and selling on the Sabbath.

Read Nehemiah 13v23-24

- They **married** people who didn't follow God.

Fit the blue words into the puzzle to see why they did this.

The yellow boxes will give the answer.

Did you know?

Sin doesn't just mean doing wrong things. Sin is thinking that <u>we</u> know better than <u>God</u>. We all want to run our own lives instead of God being our King.

The people were **still sinful**—and Nehemiah couldn't change them!

PRAY

Jesus is the **only** person who can solve the problem of sin. (*More about that tomorrow.*) Think of anything you need to say sorry to God for. Then thank God for sending Jesus so that you can be forgiven.

THE SILENCE IS BROKEN

Nehemiah was a good leader who loved God. He did a great job of rebuilding the walls of Jerusalem. But he <u>couldn't</u> rebuild the people!

*Find **Nehemiah** on your **Bible Timeline**.*

What comes next on the timeline?

400 **y**_____ of **s**_____

All through the Old Testament, God had sent **messengers** (called prophets) to speak to the Israelites.

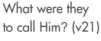

But the people stopped listening to God...

...so He stopped sending His messengers.

After 400 years, the silence was broken—in a town called Nazareth...

READ
Matthew 1v18-21

The angel told Joseph that Mary's baby was from God's Holy Spirit. What were they to call Him? (v21)

J_____

Why? (v21)

Because He will...

The name **Jesus** means:

Take the first letter of each pic.

__ __ __ __ __ __ __ __

- It tells us <u>who</u> Jesus is: He is **God**.
- And what Jesus <u>does</u>: He **saves** us.

*Turn to **God's Rescue Plan** after Day 30 to see how Jesus saves us.*

THINK + PRAY

Nehemiah couldn't rebuild people—but **Jesus** can! When we become His followers (Christians), Jesus changes us to become more and more like Him. Do you want to be like Jesus? (Loving God and other people, and keeping God's laws.) Then ask Him to change you.

DAY 61 ALL REVEALED

Welcome to the very last book in the Bible. It's called **Revelation** because it <u>reveals</u> something that was hidden.

*Use the **flag code** to see where this revelation came from.*

▥ ◩ ▬ ___ ___ ___ gave it to ▭ ▬ ▭ ◲ ▭ ___ ___ ___ ___ ___ who gave it to

◀ ▩ ▥ ▬ ◰ an ___ ___ ___ ___ ___ who gave it to ▭ ◩ ◪ ▩ ___ ___ ___ ___ .

This is in Revelation 1v1.

Did you know?

This is the same **John** who wrote John's Gospel. John was one of Jesus' disciples. His older brother James was also a disciple. Their dad was called Zebedee!

Flag Code

A=◀ D=▬ E=▬ G=▥ H=◲

I=● J=▭ L=◪ N=▩

O=◩ P=◻ S=▭ U=◲ V=⊠

John had got into trouble for telling people about Jesus. He was imprisoned on an island called Patmos. That's where he was when he wrote the book of Revelation, about the amazing things God's angel revealed to Him.

*Find **John's vision of heaven** on your Bible Timeline. (A vision is a kind of dream.)*

We're going to read the <u>last</u> part of the book of Revelation. It's all about heaven...

READ
Revelation 21v1-4

Turn to the next page to find out more.

Fill in the gaps from v1.

Then I saw a new h_____ and a new e_____.

Where do these blue words come on your **Bible Timeline**?

Beginning / Middle / End

These words are at the <u>end</u> of the timeline because Jesus will come back again one day and our world will end. John's vision shows us what that will be like.

1 John <u>saw</u> a beautiful city—the new Jerusalem. *We'll find out about that on Day 63.*

2 Then John <u>heard</u> something wonderful:

▯▯▯ ◪ ▬   ◪ ● ⊠ ▬   ▢ ▬ ▬ ◹ ◪ ▬ for ever.

_ _ _ will _ _ _ _ with His _ _ _ _ _ _ _ for ever.

3 And <u>because</u> God will be living with His people:

There will be ▦◹ _ _ death, ▦◹ _ _ mourning (sadness),

▦◹ _ _ crying and ▦◹ _ _ pain.

Wow! What a fantastic promise! No one will be sad in heaven. No one will cry.

THINK + PRAY

If you're a Christian (a follower of Jesus) then this promise is for you! **Read verse 4 again.** Which part of this promise are you looking forward to the most? Tell God why, and then thank Him for the wonderful promise of heaven.

Think of three words that begin with **A**:

A_____   A_____

A_____

And three that begin with **Z**!

Z_____   Z_____

Z_____

A and **Z** are the first and last letters in our alphabet. The first and last letters in the **Greek** alphabet are called <u>Alpha</u> and <u>Omega</u>. They look like this:

α	ω	A	Ω
Little Alpha	Little Omega	Capital Alpha	Capital Omega

John heard **God** speaking from His throne. God called <u>Himself</u> the Alpha and the Omega...

READ
Revelation 21v5-8

I am the Alpha and the Omega, the **B**_____

and the **E**_____.

God is the first and the last. He has always existed and always will. **He is the God of all time and history!**

*The rest of the verses are quite tricky. Follow the **maze** to find five hidden words. Then fit those words into the gaps to see the **XTB Xplanation**.*

Start here

e	r	i	t	t	h	e
e	r	e	h	n	i	r	i
t	e	r			h	s
r	n	i			t	r
n	l	y	a	w	a	n
a						

e _ _ _ _ _ _   i _ _ _ _ _ _

t _ _ _ _   h _ _

t _ _ _ _   a _ _ _ _

XTB Xplanation

- To those who live for God, He gives e_____ life with Him in heaven. (v6)
- Those who keep on living for God will i_____ (be given) all the things John saw in his vision. (v7)
- God will be t_____ God and they will be H_____ children. (v7)
- But those who t_____ a_____ from God will be thrown into hell. (v8)

THINK + PRAY

Are <u>you</u> a follower of Jesus?
Yes?—<u>thank God</u> for His wonderful promise of eternal life with Him in heaven. <u>Ask Him</u> to help you tell your friends about Jesus too.
Not Sure?—check out **God's Rescue Plan** after Day 30.

The angel showed John a beautiful city. *Check out the verses to see what it was like.*

The **wall** was made of j_____ (a precious stone). [Revelation 21v18]

The **city** was pure g_____ . [Revelation 21v18]

The **gates** were p_____ . [Revelation 21v21]

The city had the names of the 12 tribes of Israel, and the 12 apostles (disciples) on it. This amazing city was a picture of God's people—from Old Testament times <u>and</u> New Testament times. **All** Christians, throughout history, will be inside this city! (Revelation 21v9-21)

But some things were <u>missing</u> from the city...

READ
Revelation 21v22-27

 No t_____ (v22)

There will be no need for a special place to worship God because God the Father, and Jesus (called the Lamb), will be there with us.

 No s_____ or m_____ (v22)

The glory of God will be far brighter than any light, even the sun! This light will show God's people how He wants them to live (v23).

 G_____ never shut (v25) **No n_____**

There will be no darkness or danger or sin! Heaven will always be light and God's people will always be safe. There's no need to shut the gates because nothing impure can enter the city (v27).

But this city is just a <u>picture</u> of heaven. There will be a whole new universe. Everything will be new and more wonderful than anyone can imagine!

THINK + PRAY

Only people whose names are in the **book of life** (whose sins are forgiven by Jesus) will be there (v27). If you're a Christian, that means <u>you!</u> Thank God for this now.

At the very <u>beginning</u> of the Bible we meet these people.

Who are they?

If you're not sure, check your Bible Timeline.

Adam and Eve disobeyed God. So all people were **cursed**. They were banned from eating from the **tree of life** and from living with God for ever. (Genesis 3)

At the very <u>end</u> of the Bible, John learns something wonderful about that **curse**...

READ
Revelation 22v1-6

What did John see? (v1-2)

The __ __ __ __ __ of the __ __ __ __ __ of life.

The __ __ __ __ __ of __ __ __ __.

And what's the great news? (v3)

There will no longer be any __ __ __ __ __ __.

In heaven, God will <u>remove</u> His curse. His people will be allowed to eat from the tree of life and live for ever with Him!

• God's people will __ __ __ __ __ Him. (v3)

• They will __ __ __ His face. (v4) → *Nothing will separate God from His people.*

• His __ __ __ __ __ will be on their foreheads. (v4)
  They will belong completely to God.

• They will __ __ __ __ for ever and ever. (v5)
  They're God's servants—but they'll also rule with Him!

PRAY What a lot to thank God for...
...so start right now!

DAY 65 COMING SOON...

 xtb Revelation 22v7-21

The last 15 verses of the Bible cover a mix of things. But one important fact comes up <u>eight</u> times!

Crack the code to see what it is.

_ _ _ _ _ _ _

_ _ _ _ _ _ _ _ _

Look at the <u>end</u> of your **Timeline**.

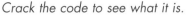

There's a dotted line at the end because we don't know <u>when</u> Jesus will come back. But we **do** know that He **will**!

Read Jesus' own words about it...

READ
Revelation 22v12-16

Jesus says there are **two** different types of people.

Spot <u>eight</u> differences in the two pics.

A: Some people have had their sins washed away by Jesus. They can enter God's city and live for ever with Him. (v14)

B: The rest continue to disobey Jesus. They will have to stay outside the city. They will be punished for ever. (v15)

THINK SPOT

Have you had your wrongs forgiven by Jesus? Will you live with Him for ever?

If you're not sure, talk to an older Christian about it. It's hugely important!

READ
Revelation 22v20-21

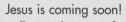

Jesus is coming soon!

THINK + PRAY

• Tell Jesus how you feel about Him coming back, and why you feel like that.
• Then ask Him to get you excited about living with Him for ever.
• And ask Him to help you to serve Him until He does come back.

TIME FOR MORE?

Have you read all 65 days of XTB? Well done if you have!

How often do you use XTB?

- Every day?
- Nearly every day?
- Two or three times a week?
- Now and then?

You can use XTB at any time...

In the morning.

At bedtime.

When you get back from school.

When do <u>you</u> read XTB?

XTB comes out every three months. If you've been using it every day, or nearly every day, that's great! You may still have a few weeks to wait before you get the next issue of XTB. But don't worry!—that's what the extra readings are for...

EXTRA READINGS

The next four pages contain extra Bible readings based on your Bible Timeline. If you read one each day, they will take you 26 days. Or you may want to read two or three each day. Or just pick a few to try. Whichever suits you best. There's a cracking wordsearch to solve too...

Drop us a line...
Why not write in and tell us what you think of XTB:

—What do you like best?
—Was there something you didn't understand?
—And any ideas for how we can make it better!

Write to: XTB, The Good Book Company, Blenheim House, 1 Blenheim Road, Epsom, Surrey, KT19 9AP, UK
or e-mail me:
alison@thegoodbook.co.uk

The extra readings start on the next page

END TO END BIBLE TIMELINE

These extra readings will whiz you through all the people and events on your Bible Timeline. Keep your timeline with you as you read, so that you can see how everything fits together...

The extra readings come from many different books in the Bible. They start with Genesis—the very first book in the Bible—and zoom all the way through to Revelation.

The ideas in the box will help you as you read the verses.

PRAY	Ask God to help you to understand what you read.
READ	Read the Bible verses, and fill in the missing word in the puzzle.
THINK	Think about what you have just read. Try to work out one main thing the writer is saying.
PRAY	Thank God for what you have learnt about Him.

There are 26 Bible readings on the next three pages. Part of each reading has been printed for you—but with a word missing. Fill in the missing words as you read the verses. Then see if you can find them all in the wordsearch below. Some are written backwards—or diagonally!

If you get stuck, check the answers at the end of Reading 26.

A	P	I	C	K	E	D	E	N	E	V	A	E	H	B
M	N	X	T	B	K	I	N	G	R	A	N	D	L	E
A	M	G	A	P	E	V	E	R	Y	T	H	I	N	G
Z	O	I	E	B	I	B	L	E	H	E	R	E	S	I
E	S	D	B	L	E	S	S	E	D	E	A	T	H	N
D	E	E	P	O	H	E	A	R	T	U	K	N	O	N
L	S	O	B	E	D	A	M	E	N	A	N	D	P	I
A	S	N	A	G	S	R	U	L	E	B	O	C	R	N
U	H	O	L	Y	D	R	E	A	M	C	W	L	A	G
G	X	T	B	P	U	C	L	O	T	H	S	O	Y	X
H	E	M	I	T	J	O	S	H	U	A	O	U	E	T
H	O	L	Y	S	P	I	R	I	T	I	N	D	D	B

Tick the box when you have read the verses.

1 ☐ **Read Genesis 1v1-5**
God made our world, our universe, and everything in them.
'In the **b** _ _ _ _ _ _ _ God created the heavens and the earth.' (v1)

2 ☐ **Read Genesis 3v1-13**
God made the first family—Adam and Eve. But they broke God's laws. This is called sin.
'The woman took some of the fruit and **a** _ _ it. She also gave some to her husband, and he ate it.' (v6)

3 ☐ **Read Genesis 6v9-22**
The people of the world were so wicked that God decided to wash it clean with a flood. God saved the only good man—Noah —and his family.
'Noah did **e** _ _ _ _ _ _ _ _ that God commanded.' (v22)

4 ☐ **Read Genesis 12v1-5**
God made three amazing promises to Abraham: 1—a huge family; 2—a land of their own; 3—someone from this family would be God's way of blessing the whole world.
'All the people on earth will be **b** _ _ _ _ _ _ through you.' (v3)

5 ☐ **Read Genesis 21v1-7**
When Abraham was 100 years old, he had the son God had promised. His son was called Isaac, which means 'he laughs'.
'Sarah said, "God has brought me laughter. Everyone who hears about this will **l** _ _ _ _ with me.' (v6)

6 ☐ **Read Genesis 25v19-26**
When Isaac grew up he became the father of twins—Esau (the hairy one!) and Jacob (the smoothie!).
'Isaac's wife could not have children, so Isaac **p** _ _ _ _ _ _ to the LORD for her.' (v21)

7 ☐ **Read Genesis 37v1-11**
Jacob had twelve sons—but Joseph was his favourite.
'Joseph had a **d** _ _ _ _ _ . When he told it to his brothers they hated him all the more.' (v5)

8 ☐ **Read Exodus 3v1-10**
The story of Joseph ends with the Israelites living in Egypt. But after 400 years, the Egyptians made them into slaves! So God chose Moses to rescue them.
'I am sending you to the king of Egypt (Pharaoh) to bring my people out of **E** _ _ _ _ .' (v10)

9 ☐ **Read Joshua 4v19-24**
After 40 years wandering in the desert, Joshua led the Israelites into the promised land of Canaan.
' The Lord did this so that all the people of the earth might **k** _ _ _ how great the LORD's power is.' (v24)

10 ☐ **Read Judges 7v19-23**

Gideon was one of the Judges who rescued the Israelites from their enemies.

'They shouted, "A sword for the LORD and for G _ _ _ _ _ ."' (v20)

11 ☐ **Read Ruth 2v11-12**

Ruth came from the country of Moab—but she married Boaz (an Israelite) and became the great-grandmother of King David!

'Ruth's son was called O _ _ _ . He was the father of Jesse, who was the father of David.' (v12)

12 ☐ **Read 1 Samuel 2v18-21**

God answered Hannah's prayer, and gave her a son—Samuel. So she gave Samuel back to God to serve Him.

'The boy S _ _ _ _ _ grew up serving the LORD.' (v21)

13 ☐ **Read 1 Samuel 10v17-25**

The Israelites demanded a king (even though <u>God</u> was their Real King!). Their first king was called Saul.

'The people shouted, "Long live the k _ _ _ !"' (v24)

14 ☐ **Read 1 Samuel 16v1-13**

When Saul turned away from God, God chose David to be the next king of Israel. David's heart was full of love for God.

'People look at the outward appearance, but the LORD looks at the h _ _ _ _ .' (v7)

15 ☐ **Read 1 Kings 3v5-14**

David's son, Solomon, asked God for wisdom so that he could rule the Israelites well.

'Without wisdom it is impossible to r _ _ _ this great people of yours.' (v9)

16 ☐ **Read Daniel 6v16-23**

Daniel trusted and obeyed God—even when it meant being thrown to the lions!

'My God sent His a _ _ _ _ to shut the mouths of the lions.' (v22)

17 ☐ **Read Esther 4v12-16**

Esther was a Jewish girl who became queen of Persia. She risked her life to save the rest of the Jews from an evil plot.

'You may have been chosen queen for just such a t _ _ _ as this.' (v14)

18 ☐ **Read Nehemiah 2v1-6**

Like Esther, Nehemiah also risked the king's anger to help his fellow Jews (Israelites).

'I prayed to the God of h _ _ _ _ _ .' (v4)

19 ☐ **Read Luke 2v1-7**

Jesus was born in Bethlehem—the town David had been born in 1000 years earlier.

'Mary wrapped the baby in c _ _ _ _ _ and laid Him in a manger.' (v7)

20 ☐ **Read Matthew 3v13-17**

When Jesus was baptised by John the Baptist, God voice was heard. God called Jesus His loved Son.

'This is my S _ _ whom I love.' (v17)

This is my Son.

21 ☐ **Read John 5v1-9**

Jesus did amazing miracles. He healed sick people, stopped a storm by speaking to it, and even brought dead people back to life!

'At once the man was cured. He p _ _ _ _ _ up his mat and walked.' (v9)

22 ☐ **Read Matthew 7v24-29**

Jesus' teaching is hugely important. Not obeying His words is as disastrous as your house falling down!

'The crowds were a _ _ _ _ _ _ at His teaching.' (v28)

23 ☐ **Read Matthew 28v1-10**

When Jesus died on the cross it was not the end—because God brought Him back to life again!

'He is not h _ _ _ ; He has risen, just as He said He would.' (v6)

24 ☐

Read Acts 1v9-11

Jesus went up (ascended) into heaven. One day He will come back again.

'Jesus was taken up before their very eyes, and a c _ _ _ _ hid Him from their sight.' (v9)

25 ☐ **Read Acts 2v1-13**

When the first Christians were given the Holy Spirit, He helped them to tell others all about Jesus.

'They were all filled with the H _ _ _ S _ _ _ _ _ and began to talk in other languages.' (v4)

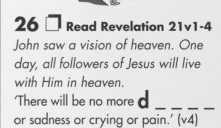

26 ☐ **Read Revelation 21v1-4**

John saw a vision of heaven. One day, all followers of Jesus will live with Him in heaven.

'There will be no more d _ _ _ _ or sadness or crying or pain.' (v4)

WHAT NEXT?

Now that you've finished this issue of XTB, why not try one of the other issues. There are twelve to choose from...

XTB 1: The Book of Beginnings
(Genesis, Matthew, Acts)

XTB 2: Miracles and Dreams
(Genesis, Matthew, Acts)

XTB 3: Comings and Goings
(Exodus, Matthew, Acts)

XTB 4: Travels Unravelled
(Exodus, Matthew, Acts)

XTB 5: The Promise Keeper
(Numbers, Mark, Ephesians)

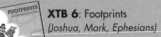

XTB 6: Footprints
(Joshua, Mark, Ephesians)

XTB 7: Heroes and Zeros
(Judges, Ruth, Mark)

XTB 8: The Real King
(1 Samuel, Mark, Psalms)

XTB 9: Way to Go
(2 Samuel, John)

XTB 10: Check It Out
(1 Kings, 2 Kings, John)

XTB 11: Write and Wrong
(2 Kings, Isaiah, Jeremiah, John)

XTB 12: End to End
(Daniel, Nehemiah, John, Revelation)

Look out for the three seasonal editions of XTB too: *Christmas Unpacked, Easter Unscrambled* and *Summer Signposts*.

*Or maybe try **Discover:** Bible notes for young people. They'll help you build on what you've learned with XTB.*

XTB and Discover are available from your local Christian bookshop—or one of the web addresses on Page 1.

XTB Joke Page

Why did the chicken cross the road?
I don't know—ask the chicken!

What's black and white and red all over?
A newspaper!

I felt like having 50 chocolate cakes in the morning.
What did you feel like in the afternoon?
Sick!

Why did the elephant bring toilet paper to the party?
Because he was a party pooper!

Why did the boy eat his homework?
Because he thought it was a piece of cake!

Patient: Doctor, Doctor, I can't get to sleep.
Doctor: Lie on the end of the bed and you'll soon drop off!

All sent in by Emily Fawcett.

Do you have any questions?

...about anything you've read in XTB?
—send them in and we'll do our best to answer them.

Write to: XTB, The Good Book Company, Blenheim House, 1 Blenheim Road, Epsom, Surrey, KT19 9AP, UK **or email me:** alison@thegoodbook.co.uk